The Zen of Passing the Bar Exam

The Zen of Passing the Bar Exam

Chad Noreuil

Clinical Professor of Law
Sandra Day O'Connor College of Law
Arizona State University

Carolina Academic Press
Durham, North Carolina

Library of Congress Cataloging-in-Publication Data
Noreuil, Chad.
The zen of passing the bar exam / Chad Noreuil.
p. cm.
Includes index.
ISBN 978-1-59460-934-3 (alk. paper)
1. Bar examinations--United States. I. Title.

KF303.N69 2010
340.076--dc22

2010032011

Carolina Academic Press
700 Kent Street
Durham, NC 27701
Telephone (919) 489-7486
Fax (919) 493-5668
www.cap-press.com
www.caplaw.com

2016 Printing
Printed in the United States of America

FOR ZEN

... the love of my life, my heart & soul,
my inspiration, my greatest teacher, my son.

Special thanks to Amy Levine, Jenny Bishop, Marie Ann Lambert, Maddi Vera, Harmony Simmons, Ben Herbert, Beth DiFelice, Shannon Mataele and Natasha Ter-Grigoryan for all of your efforts in helping make this book become a reality. Thank you all!

Contents

Introduction

When the student is ready,
the teacher will appear.

Since 2003, I have been tutoring for the bar exam. I currently lecture nationally for BarBri bar review, and I also teach seminars throughout the country on the topics covered in this book. About the time I started tutoring for the bar exam, I began to notice the many parallels between how one should approach the bar exam, and how Zen principles teach one to approach life. I incorporated many of these principles into my tutoring, and the results have been incredible. I've written this book to reach an even larger audience, in the hope that others might also be helped on the path to passing the bar exam.

Zen is a way of life—and so is passing the bar exam. I have written this book to offer a comprehensive way to approach studying for (and passing) the bar exam. In Zen, the ultimate goal is to reach enlightenment (or nirvana). As for the bar exam, the ultimate goal is passing. Accordingly, throughout the book I liken the end goal of enlightenment of Zen with the end goal of the "enlightenment" of passing the bar exam.

In each section, I offer a Zen quote[1] to introduce concepts that can be applied to studying for the bar exam in order to maximize your chances of passing. I truly believe that this approach is, for many, the best approach to passing the exam. Buddhism is about balance, knowing yourself, knowing your universe, and staying focused on the path to enlightenment. Similarly, these principles should be the foundation for maximizing your chances of passing the bar exam.

In addition to offering a comprehensive approach to studying, I also offer specific, practical advice for doing well on both the essay and MBE portions of the bar exam. I hope you enjoy reading this book as much as I enjoyed writing it. Enjoy your path to enlightenment.

The journey of a thousand miles must begin with a single step....

---

1. Several of the quotes have been passed down from Zen Masters through the years and have no attribution; a handful of quotes/stories are from Daniel Levin's *The Zen Book* (which I highly recommend); and other quotes I have attributed where appropriate.

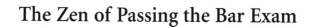

The Zen of Passing the Bar Exam

1. Preparing for the Journey

The root of all suffering
is not accepting things the way they are.

I remember being somewhat bitter about having to study for the bar exam—as if three years of law school hazing wasn't enough. Almost immediately after celebrating graduation, one's thoughts (and accompanying anxieties, fears, and dread) immediately turn to the looming bar exam. Now you are forced to learn (or re-learn) a LOT of law in a relatively short amount of time, and if you don't pass— all of that debt you accumulated over the last three years is basically for nothing. It's enough to make anyone bitter.[2]

The first lesson of Zen: if you do not accept the way things are, you will experience some degree of suffering. And, as you might have guessed, experiencing a state of suffering is not the best place to begin your path toward the enlightenment of passing the bar exam. Accept each situation as it is, and you can be at peace. When you are at peace, there are no distractions, no roadblocks along your path. The harder you resist something, the more it will push back— and the monster known as the bar exam has the potential to push back pretty hard.

In Zen, no circumstance is right or wrong, good or bad—it just is. But if you are not of the Zen-mind yet, and you are looking for a silver lining, studying for the bar exam gives you the opportunity to actually learn all of the things that you forgot immediately after your first-year final exams. It will also provide you an opportunity for self-discovery, for when we are truly challenged, we are given the chance to know our true self.

Our life is shaped by our mind; we become what we think.
— the Buddha

So what is it that you want to become? Someone who passes the bar exam or someone who doesn't? In my humble opinion, having a positive mental outlook is the single most important thing you can do in order to pass the bar exam. Numerous studies have shown that

---

2. The National Conference of Bar Examiners accurately notes that the purpose of having a bar exam requirement is to protect the public from incompetent representation.

optimists learn more effectively and efficiently than non-optimists (including, but not limited to, "pessimists") and perform better on tests, on job performance, etc.[3]

Whatever you have to do to remain positive, do it. Believe you will pass; start telling yourself every single day that you will pass; put notes up around your house reminding you to stay positive; visualize yourself opening the letter from the Bar Examiners telling you that you passed. I cannot guarantee that you will pass if you do this. But I can guarantee that your likelihood of success is much higher by being positive and believing you will pass than by being negative and having doubts. Become what you think—think (believe!) that you will pass, and you will pass.

But how do you stay positive and motivated during what could be considered (by the non-Zen mind) to be a grueling process? Why are you taking the exam in the first place? A better life for you? A better life for your kids? To help people? To make a lot of money? Remind yourself of why you went to law school in the first place—that may help. If not, find other motivations. Have gratitude that you have attained a position in life where you are preparing to take the bar exam—the precipice of an incredible achievement. Draw from this and stay positive as much as you can. As Daniel Levin so adeptly notes in *The Zen Book*: Why do we think that it's only the things that we do that matter and not the things we think?

Live each moment in gratitude for all that is.

---

3. *See* Sarath A. Nonis, et al., *Changes in College Student Composition and Implications for Marketing Education: Revisiting Predictors of Academic Success*, 58 J. Bus. Res. 321, 327 (2005) (results show successful students exhibit high level of drive and optimism); Rachel Seginer, *Defensive Pessimism and Optimism Correlates of Adolescent Future Orientation*, 15 J. Adolescent Res. 307, 317 (2000) (optimism had positive links with the motivational component of prospective education); *see generally*, Martin Seligman, *Learned Optimism: How to Change Your Mind and Your Life*, Pocket Books (1998); Peter Schulman, *Applying Learned Optimism to Increase Sales Productivity*, 19 J. Pers. Selling & Sales Mgmt. 31 (1999) (expectation that one will succeed affects performance).

Zen is about being present — about having gratitude for all that is. Granted, given the nature of the beast you are about to confront, having gratitude (or keeping a positive mental outlook) can be a difficult task. Here is something I tell my students before final exams: at its most fundamental level, life always boils down to two perspectives — "Get To" or "Have To." Everything you do can be compartmentalized into these two categories. The more you choose to place your perspective in the "get to" column, the better your attitude will be (and, as we have already seen, a positive attitude is a definite factor in maximizing the effectiveness of your study time).

At some point, you may find yourself saying that you "have to" study for the bar exam. Those who have been denied admittance to law school (or those who have flunked out or withdrawn) would likely say you "get to" take the exam (while they do not). Taking the exam is a privilege — one which you had to trudge through three years of law school to earn. Remind yourself that you don't "**have to**" study — you "**get to**" study because you are afforded the opportunity to see, to read, to understand. The more you appreciate this fact (and everything else in your life), the more balanced you will be, and the more likely it is that you will reach your ultimate goal of passing the bar exam.

Zen is not a pastime, but the most serious task in life.
No empty head will ever venture near it.
— Zen Master D.T. Suzuki

Similarly, studying for the bar exam cannot be viewed as a pastime. It, too, is one of the most serious tasks of your life. (And, after three years of law school, I'm sure you do not have an "empty head.") In Zen, to truly reach enlightenment, you must (in most cases) change your way of thinking, your way of being, your way of life. Such is the case with achieving the enlightenment of the bar exam — you must change your way of life. You must have more focus and concentration, you must be more disciplined, you must adjust your personal relationships, and you must adjust your diet. Be simple. Approach the bar exam as if it's your full-time job.

Your Personal Relationships During the Bar Exam

It's probably a good idea to tell friends and family that you may not have time to hang out with them or return calls during the lead-up to the bar exam. The bar exam is tough enough without having drama with family and friends, so explain to them the rigorous study demands that you'll be forced to endure and ask for support.

Moreover, explain the importance of the exam, as some non-lawyers may not even realize that you cannot practice law until you pass the bar exam. Finally, it may be a good idea to apologize in advance if you appear stressed out when you do interact with family and friends. (Of course, if you have a Zen-mind, this will not happen.)

If friends and family miss you too much, get them involved: ask them to help you. This may be in the form of cooking a few meals, doing your laundry, or even helping you study. Some of you learn best by talking through things, so consider having your significant other act as a sounding board for your recitation of rules, or perhaps have him/her go through flashcards with you.

When you are with people,
be 100 percent with them;
when you are by yourself,
be 100 percent alone. This is the
way of all things: Be exactly where
you are at any given moment and
everything will be without strain.

Your time will be limited with friends and family, it's important to remember that you will need to take breaks from studying and spend time with loved ones. When you do this, do it completely — do your best to suspend thoughts of studying and focus on the time you are spending with friends or family. In this way, you have another opportunity to practice being present.

Lifestyle During the Bar Exam

In addition to your personal relationships, your lifestyle will be a significant factor in whether you pass the bar exam. Diet, exercise, and adequate sleep are key factors to having your brain function at its optimal level. If you're thinking about glossing over this section, please don't. It may be more important than anything you learn in a bar review prep class. First—your diet.

Buddhist monks primarily eat vegetables and rice. They understand that when the body feels bad, it is more difficult to focus on the path. Eating well (mostly) assures that the way your physical body feels will not inhibit your focus and concentration. The nutrients (or lack thereof) you ingest are the primary factors in determining how well or how poorly your immune system functions[4]—and you certainly don't want to become ill during the lead-up to the bar exam.

Moreover, it's critical to eat healthy, well-balanced meals in order to maximize your ability to learn (e.g., process and retain information). Eat all natural foods (fruits, vegetables, whole grains, lean proteins, etc.) and cut out processed foods and sugar as much as possible. Sugar in particular can have a deleterious effect on brain function,[5] as can too much caffeine.[6]

Conversely, incorporate some Omega 3 and/or Omega 6 Fatty Acids into your diet (most commonly found in fish, such as salmon). If you don't like fish, there are a variety of supplements

---

4. Susanna Cunningham-Rundles, *Nutrition and Immune Function*, 1 FRONTIERS IN NUTRITIONAL SCI. 21 (2002).

5. 5 Jane A. Goldman, et al., *Behavioral Effects of Sucrose on Preschool Children*, 14 J. ABNORMAL CHILD PSYCHOL. 565 (1986) (study found objective evidence in young children of a significant time-dependent behavior effect of sucrose ingestion).

6. BBC.news.com, *Caffeine 'Reduces Productivity,'* January 29, 2001, http://news.bbc.co/uk/2/hi/health/1142492.stm (study found high caffeine intake leads to dehydration that coupled with stimulating effects of caffeine causes detrimental effect on concentration).

that you can take. Recent studies have shown that Omega 3 fatty acids improve brain function—especially memory.[7] Salmon, mackerel, herring, trout, tuna, and halibut are rich in Omega 3 fatty acids.

It's a Marathon, Not a Sprint

No one reaches enlightenment in a day. Similarly, no one passes the bar exam (or is prepared to pass the bar exam) in a single day. Don't think about how far away (or how close) the actual test is— just be present in each moment.

Also, part of the process is making sure you take a break every now and then. A run-down body and mind is not optimal for learning. Accordingly, be sure to take a break at regular intervals—both throughout the day, and by taking a day/night off every now and then. Hopefully, you can come back to your study schedule refreshed and focused.

It is the readiness of the mind
that is true wisdom....

❷   ❷   ❷

---

7. *See* S. Yehuda, S. Rabinovitz, & D.I. Mostofsky, *Essential Fatty Acids and the Brain: From Infancy to Aging*, 26 Neurobiology of Aging S98, S100 (2005) ("In general, EFA [essential fatty acids] improves learning and memory.") citing S. Yehuda, S. Rabinovitz, R.L. Carasso, & D.I. Mostofsky, *Mixture of Essential Fatty Acids Rehabilitates Stress Effects on Learning, and Cortisol and Cholesterol Level*, 101 Int'l J. Neuroscience 73–87 (2000); John Hopkins Health Alerts, *Eating Fish May Help Preserve Your Memory (Along with Your Heart) and Protect Against Alzheimer's Disease*, June 13, 2006, http://www.johnshopkins healthalerts.com/alerts/nutrition_weight_control/JohnsHopkinsNutrition WeightControlHealthAlert_208-1.html (recent study found eating fish with Omega 3 fatty acids twice a week reduces the risk of developing Alzheimer's disease by seventy percent).

2. Knowing Your True Self

He who knows others is wise.
He who knows himself is enlightened.

— Lao Tzu (from the Tao Te Ching)

Zen is about knowing the true nature of yourself (and, ultimately, the true "oneness" of the universe). In order to pass the bar exam, it is critical to know yourself: What kind of learner are you? What is the best way you process and assimilate mountains of information? Do you have trouble focusing? Are you someone who experiences test anxiety? Knowing the answers to these questions will go a long way to help you prepare for the bar exam. If you have never asked yourself the questions I have posed above, I invite you to do so now. Be present—turn inward and make contact with the inner you who knows all of the answers.

Of all the questions posed above, the most important may be what kind of learner you are. After all, passing the bar exam depends in large part on learning (and retaining) massive amounts of information. Of course, we are all a combination of learners, but some are more visual, others more auditory, etc. After your 20 years (or more) of school, hopefully you have some idea of what type of learner you are. If not, experiment. See what works best for you. Try flashcards, audiotapes, explaining rules of law to your significant other, memorizing your outline while walking, etc.

If you are really at a loss as to what type of learner you are, there are various websites you can go to in order to figure it out.[8] Of course, oftentimes, a combination of the above may work best for you. We are all a combination of learning styles, but almost everyone has a predominant way in which s/he learns best. Knowing yourself in this way will ensure you are studying in the most efficient and effective manner.

What Type of Essay Writer Are You?

Whoever knows himself knows God.
— Muhammad

---

8. Grace Fleming, About.com, Learning Style Quiz: Visual, Kinesthetic, and Auditory Styles, http://homeworktips.about.com/od/homeworkhelp/a/lstyleqz. htm (last visited May 5, 2010); http://www.ldpride.net/learningstyles.MI.htm (last visited May 5, 2010).

As a corollary to the above questions, knowing yourself for the bar exam involves an even deeper question: What type of essay writer are you? Again, the Zen path to enlightenment largely turns on understanding your true nature. And knowing your true nature is imperative to passing the bar exam. Unfortunately, we often fail to self-analyze when preparing for a major task, such as the bar exam.

As part of this introspection, it's important to know what kind of essay writer you are. Take a look at the examples below. These are the three most common ways examinees answer questions on the bar exam—but only one of them will maximize your score. Recognizing different types of answers will help you avoid falling into similar patterns that undermine many bar essay scores.

For this exercise, assume the definition for first-degree murder is "the unlawful killing of another with malice aforethought and causation." I've given a fact pattern that is merely one small part of an overall question, as indicated by the word "partial" in the title. As such, the "answers" below the fact pattern are partial as well. See if you can pick out the "best" answer of the three.

Example 2-1
Partial Fact Pattern — Criminal Law Essay

Bob is showing off his new gun to Ted. Thinking there are no bullets in the gun, Bob reenacts a scene from his favorite movie—points the gun at Ted and pulls the trigger, hitting and killing Ted. With what crimes can Bob be convicted? Please evaluate fully, including any and all defenses that may apply.

ANSWER #1 (PARTIAL)

First-degree murder
First-degree murder is the intentional killing of another with malice aforethought and causation. One acts with malice aforethought when he acts knowingly and purposefully. Here, although Bob was the actual and proximate

cause of Ted's death, he had no malice aforethought (e.g., he didn't act knowingly and/or purposefully). Thus, he cannot be guilty of first-degree murder.

ANSWER #2 (PARTIAL)

First-degree murder

First-degree murder is the intentional killing of another with malice aforethought and causation. One acts with malice aforethought when he acts knowingly and purposefully. Here, Bob was only "showing off his new gun to Ted." When reenacting a scene from his favorite movie, Bob pointed the gun at Ted and pulled the trigger, killing Ted. However, Bob did not think there were any bullets in the gun. Therefore, Bob cannot be guilty of first-degree murder.

ANSWER #3 (PARTIAL)

First-degree murder

First-degree murder is the intentional killing of another with malice aforethought (acting knowingly and purposefully) and causation. Here, Bob killed another because Ted died. Also, Bob satisfies the causation requirement because but for his act of pointing the gun at Ted and pulling the trigger, Ted would not have died. However, Bob did not act with malice aforethought (did not act knowingly and/or purposefully) because he did not think there were any bullets in the gun. Thus, Bob had no intent to kill Ted and cannot be guilty of first-degree murder.

Okay—these answers are the types that I typically see from examinees. Can you identify which category of essay writer you fall into? Let's discuss all three answers and figure out which is the better model.

ANSWER #1: The Law-Based Answer

Upon first reading, #1 seems to be on target, right? It first lays out the correct rule of law, and appears at first glance to analyze various parts of the rule, then correctly concludes. But when we look more closely, we can see its flaws.

This answer represents what I call the "law-based" answer. This type of answer gives the rule of law, and then makes a conclusion about the various parts of the rule (elements or factors) without giving specific facts to support those conclusions.

Specifically, what we have in Answer #1 is a conclusion about one of the elements, another conclusion about another element, and then a final conclusion — none of which are supported by any FACTS. Thus, in actuality, the answer is completely devoid of analysis (on paper, anyway). There can be no analysis without application of specific facts to specific parts of the rule!

This is a classic example (and mistake) of not showing all of your work. The writer is clearly going through all the steps in his/her head, but it doesn't show on paper. To the grader, the writer could just as easily be guessing at each conclusion. Accordingly, your score is not going to be as high as it could be — despite reaching the correct conclusion.

As an aside, you'll notice that Answer #1 has two sentences for the "Rule" portion of the essay. If there are terms that need to be defined in the broader rule, then define them. Here, malice aforethought is one of those terms, and if you want to save time, you can do so with a parenthetical definition after the term (as is indicated in Answer #3).

ANSWER #2: The Fact-Based Answer

This answer is what I call the "fact-based" answer. Again, at first blush, the answer may appear to be a good one. The issue is given, the rule is given, and then the relevant facts are noted. As in Answer #1, this answer also concludes correctly.

However, the answer has no specific factual application to any part of the rule. This is not analysis either. Despite noting the material facts upon which the issue turns, there is not integration of fact and law (which equals "analysis"). I believe I have said it before but I will say it again: THERE CAN BE NO ANALYSIS WITHOUT AN APPLICATION OF FACT TO LAW.

ANSWER #3: The Integrated Answer

Answer #3 is a much better answer. As a disclaimer, I will note, that there are many answers that could be written differently and still get full point value. All I am saying is that Answer #3 is far better than #s 1 and 2 because it actually gives an analysis. This is what the Bar Examiners want—the ability to discern which facts meet or negate each element of the rule.

Answer #3 is an example of an answer that SHOWS ALL OF THE WORK. It lays out all of the steps that the examinee went through in his/her head. Remember—you have to put it down on paper to maximize your points.

Though #3 is slightly longer than the other two, you will ultimately save time by writing in this template because you will know exactly what you are looking for and exactly how to put it down on paper. (The more you practice, the more efficient you will become.) And, most importantly, the integrated answer will maximize your score.

Do not go after the past,
Nor lose yourself in the future.
For the past no longer exists,
And the future is not yet here.
By looking deeply at things just as they are,
In this moment, here and now,
The seeker lives calmly and freely.
— Bhaddekaratta Sutra

Because the analysis is such a vital part of doing well on the bar exam, I want to provide you a more in-depth opportunity to look more deeply at who you truly are as an essay writer before we move on. Below, I have listed a short fact pattern and the applicable rule of law governing the issue I would like you to focus on: the dying declaration hearsay exception from evidence. Please read carefully—practice being present.

<u>Relevant fact pattern</u>:
During a criminal trial against John Smith, the prosecution seeks to introduce a 911 audio recording of a phone call to a police dispatcher. The voice on the recording calmly states, "This is Abby. My husband has just stabbed me. He has been embezzling money from his company, and he has killed me because I know too much." Abby was later found unconscious and is in a coma at the time of trial. Is the 911 call admissible at trial?

<u>Relevant rule (dying declaration hearsay exception)</u>:
A statement made by a now unavailable declarant is admissible if:
(1) the declarant believed her death was imminent, and
(2) the statement concerned the cause of what she believed to be her impending death.

You now have the relevant rule and the relevant facts required to answer this issue. I invite you to take about five minutes (that's all it should take) and write out an answer. This is part of reinforcing the learning process (active learning). So I encourage you to fight the urge to forgo this step, and write out a quick answer. It's only five minutes, and it's a step on the road to passing the bar exam. Remember—there are no short cuts on the path to enlightenment. After you are done, turn the page and take a look at the model answers.

☯   ☯   ☯

Example 2-2 (ANSWER #1 to Dying Declaration)

Dying Declaration

A statement made by a now unavailable declarant is admissible if: (1) the declarant believed her death was imminent (but need not actually die), and (2) the statement concerned the cause of what she believed to be her impending death. The reason for the rule is because it is thought that people on their death beds are not likely to tell lies.

Here, Abby is unavailable to testify at trial. Also, she made the relevant statement while truly believing her death was imminent. Also, the statement specifically concerned the cause of her death. Thus, all elements are met and Abby's statements will be admissible at trial under the dying declaration hearsay exception.

How does your answer match up with this one? Hopefully, your answer isn't at all similar. Again, the answer above is one with a "false analysis"—one devoid of fact application. Although changed slightly, this answer is from an actual student I tutored. It was clear that s/he knew the analysis—but again, failed to show all of the work on paper.

One other important point—take note of the last sentence in the "rule" paragraph in Answer #1: "The reason for the rule is because it is thought that people on their death beds are not likely to tell lies." While this is true, it is superfluous and a great example of a time waster. The Bar Examiners do not want to know all of the historical information you know about a particular issue/topic. Your job is to answer the specific question asked by noting issues, giving applicable rules, applying facts to rules, and concluding. Period. Your job is difficult enough without adding superfluous verbiage.

Here is a re-write of how the answer would look in an integrated fact-rule format (while also maximizing your score):

Example 2-3 (ANSWER #2 to Dying Declaration)

<u>Dying Declaration</u>

A statement made by a now unavailable declarant is admissible if: (1) the declarant believed her death was imminent (but need not actually die), and (2) the statement concerned the cause of what she believed to be her impending death.

Here, Abby is unavailable to testify because she is in a coma. Also, she believed death to be imminent because she said her husband "has killed me...." Furthermore, the statement concerned the cause of what she believed to be her impending death because she said "my husband has just stabbed me." Thus, the dying declaration exception will apply and the statement will be admissible at trial.

Does you answer look more like Answer #2? Hopefully, it does. Answer #2 is much better at applying specific facts to specific parts of the rule. Another way of putting it — each "sub-conclusion" is supported by a fact. The grader knows that the writer is not merely guessing at each conclusion because the writer in Answer #2 showed all of her work.

Another important point about Answer #2 lies in the quoting of Abby's words. Whenever the bar puts statements in quotes, it's always a good idea for you to do the same. If the fact pattern quotes someone's words, you can be assured that those words are important to the analysis. Moreover, quoting specific words forces you to match up facts with parts of the rule.

At this point, I hope you have been able to identify what type of essay writer you are. Oftentimes, I find that students go through all of law school and have never been told how to "show all of their work" to ensure they are giving an integrated, well-reasoned analysis. Once you have identified the true nature of what type of essay writer you are, you can take steps to improve your essay writing. If you would like additional practice, I have listed additional short exercises in Appendix C (with model answers and discussions after each).

Your work is to discover your world
and then with all your heart
give yourself to it.
— the Buddha

3. Your Presence is Requested ...

When you walk, walk;
when you eat, eat; and
when you sit, sit.
This is the way of Zen.
Do what you do fully in each moment.

Zen is all about being present—being mindful of every single thing you do. The more mindful you can be in everyday mundane activities, the further you will be on your path to enlightenment. The more you practice being mindful in your everyday activities, the more your brain will be trained to concentrate on the task at hand—and the more efficient you will be in studying and retaining information.

So ask yourself: how "present" are you throughout the day? Are you mindful and fully immersed in what you are doing, or are you constantly having thoughts about the past ("I can't believe she said that") or the future ("I wonder what I should eat for dinner")? When you wash your hands, are you present? Are you mindful of the water's temperature, of how it feels against your hands? Or are you thinking about what you're going to do next? The more you practice being mindful, the closer you will be to enlightenment. Thus, when you sit to study, you will study with a mindful focus.

In Zen, the path to enlightenment requires many hours a day of intense meditation—which can be described as the practice of being present. Similarly, passing the bar exam requires hours of intense meditation of a different kind. In Zen Buddhism, *zazen* (literally meaning "seated meditation") is a meditative discipline practitioners perform to calm the body and the mind to experience the insight of (among other things) being present. Zen meditation is normally always the same—to the relative positioning of the body, to the sequence of one's breathing, to how to deal with the thoughts that will inevitably pop up in one's mind.

How you approach studying should also be the same every time. One approach might be to first review your outlines (or flashcards, etc.) for a particular subject, and then advance to practice essays, and then to MBE questions (or some combination thereof). Of course, be sure to incorporate regular breaks into your schedule, too. It is usually helpful to study in the same place, at the same time of day (the brain learns best when it is conditioned to study at the same time), under the same conditions.

Moreover, the process of how you "practice" for the bar exam should be the same every time. For example, the process of how you answer essay questions should be the same each time. Once the process becomes second nature, the brain is more free to concentrate on the task at hand. So, for essays, what is the process you should undertake each time?

At the outset, I wouldn't suggest doing practice essays until you know the law on a given subject. Otherwise, it could just be a waste of time. When you feel well-versed on a particular subject, then you can start writing practice essays.

To get the most out of your practice essays, be sure to do every essay under test conditions. This means doing practice essays without any distractions—no phone, no TV, no snacking, no pets sitting on your lap. And, as best you can, try to focus on the task at hand as if it were the real thing. The more you can "practice" and train your brain under simulated test conditions, the more you will be prepared to do well on exam day.

Keep track of your time on every practice essay. Only do essays under the same time pressures you will have for the exam. Write down your start time and finish time for every essay. This will give you a gauge for each subject as to how you are doing (and if you need to cut down on your time). It will also give you an idea as to which specific subjects you finish on time and which you have trouble completing within thirty minutes.

At first, it's okay to go over your allotted thirty minutes when doing practice essays. Write until you are done. This will give you a more accurate gauge of your timing. Moreover, it will give you the full amount of practice you need. Perhaps you will find that you are always under thirty minutes on Torts, but always over on time on Contracts. Knowing this information may prove invaluable on the day of the exam.

Writing the answer, however, is only the first part of your practice. The other part is in reviewing the model answers. If you take a bar review course (or buy the books), every essay will have a model answer. (If you just practice with old released exams, there are usually model answers or at least "issue summaries" available for your review.)

Take the time to note each issue, each rule, and each fact application. Figure out where you are deficient. Are you having more problems with issue spotting, or with giving the full rules of applicable law? Again—knowing yourself is key to attaining the ultimate enlightenment of passing the bar exam.

Having set up the parameters for your practice, we can now discuss the specifics. The specific way you approach answering each essay (similar to a zazen meditation) should be the same each time.

Read the Call of the Question First

One of the most important pieces of advice for doing well on an essay is to read the call of the question first. The "call" of the question is the part that "calls" for you to answer a specific (or general) question. The call is almost always located in the last paragraph of the fact pattern (and often the last sentence). The call of the question is the most important part of essay writing—because you will be asked something specific here, and you need to respond specifically.

Moreover, if you read the call of the question FIRST, you will be grounded in the subject matter. This will put you in a "Torts frame of mind" (if, of course, it's a Torts question) and give better context to the fact pattern. This is important because you may not know UNTIL the call of the question what the actual subject is—a Torts question could look like a property question, which could look like a contracts question, which could look like a business organizations question, and so forth and so on.

Below is an example of a typical opening fact pattern for a bar exam essay question. See if you can recognize the subject being tested. The first is from the February 2004 Arizona Bar Exam, Question #9:

> You and your spouse are having dinner at the home of Susan Swensen, president of Sweets Corp. ("Sweets"). Sweets, which is one of your biggest clients, is in the business of operating retail sweets shops in shopping malls. While Mr. Swensen, Susan's husband, is passing around

dessert, Susan says, "That reminds me," and begins to tell about a plan that she has just hatched.

Susan intends to enter into a contract with Patrick Pete, owner of 51% of the outstanding shares of Pete's Treats, Inc. ("Pete's Treats"). Pete's Treats, the largest competitor of Sweets, is owned by a total of eight shareholders.

Okay, we're two paragraphs into the fact pattern and there is still no indication as to what subject we're dealing with. At first, you see the words "you and your spouse," which might lead you into thinking Family Law (or Community Property) may be on the horizon. Then you see words such as "Corp." and "51% of the outstanding shares of Pete's Treats, Inc." and you might think it would be a Corporations/Business Organizations question. And of course, anytime you see something about a "plan" being "hatched" you most likely begin to think about Criminal Law. Finally, the first sentence of paragraph #2 invokes contracts with the "intends to enter into a contract" language.

So which subject is being tested? Answer: none of them. This is actually a Professional Responsibility question. This, of course, is made perfectly clear by the call of the question, which starts off with the words, "[p]lease discuss the legal and professional responsibility issues raised by Susan's plan...." As you can see, reading the call of the question first will help you in several ways.

After Reading the Call of the Question ...

After you read the call of the question, read the fact pattern with the call in mind. Digest facts and look for issues. If you are comfortable doing so, jot down issues in the margins. Read slowly, read carefully, and read critically. Keep in mind that (1) **most every fact matters,** and (2) **issues always come from facts.** I recommend reading the fact pattern twice. At the end, be sure to read the call of the question a second time. It is absolutely crucial to answer the specific question asked (rather than giving a "brain dump" of everything you know about a particular topic).

At this point, I'm often asked—should I outline or should I just start writing? Like any good answer to a good law school question, the answer is: It depends. If you become adept at jotting down issues or other notes as you read the facts, this could replace your "outline" for each question. Outlining your answer ahead of time also depends on how comfortable you feel with the time constraints. You should know this if you've done enough practice essays—are you usually short on time? If so, outlining might not be the best thing for you. The key is to find what works for you (know yourself) and practice accordingly.

When asked one time,
"What is the highest dharma (duty) a man can offer in service
of mankind?" Buddha responded, "Chopping wood
and carrying water." The practice of Zen is not about lofty
lectures and philosophical teaching, but rather, it's the
simple awareness of everyday life.

Writing out practice essays is similar to chopping wood. It doesn't seem as if it's such an important thing, but it is. The key is to appreciate the everyday chopping of wood (studying, writing out practice essays) and bring your awareness to that task. Be present in writing out your essays—and chop your wood the same way each time. After reading the call of the question, reading the fact pattern and spotting issues (and perhaps outlining or jotting down notes as described above), you are ready to start chopping wood. Enlightenment is always about the journey.

Writing the Essay

Contrary to what you may believe, you can know every aspect of every rule of law, and still do poorly on the bar exam. Passing most often depends on not only knowing the law, but also knowing how to take the bar exam. First, it's essential to know how to write bar exam essays in order to maximize your score.

Many of my tutorees who have failed the bar (I only tutor those who have previously not passed) often tell me that they studied twelve hours a day and knew every single rule of law (and thus couldn't believe they failed). And, in fact, most of them truly did know most all of the law that was tested, but they didn't put their analyses down on paper in a way that maximized their points.

Most likely, you are going to be pressed for time when writing your essay answers, so you want to write in a format that both maximizes your points and is efficient. Have a Zen-mind and keep it simple. Know exactly how you are going to attack your essay answers, and use that approach every single time. Whenever possible, plug into a template for each topic—have an organizational framework for each answer.

Usually, an IRAC or CRAC (conclusion first) is a good starting place for writing your bar essay answers. The IRAC framework may be oversimplified for the practice of law (or even, some would argue, for a law school exam), but on the time-pressured bar exam, IRAC works well. Other organizational frameworks can be just as effective, but you cannot go wrong with IRAC as your starting point for organizing your essay answer.

The biggest mistake examinees make in writing is within their analyses (the "A" of IRAC). We all know that "analysis" is supposed to be the application of facts to rules. This is certainly true—but I am amazed at how many people do this incorrectly. (By "incorrectly" I mean writing in a way that fails to maximize their score.)

Knowing how to analyze the law vis-à-vis a fact pattern (often referred to as "logical reasoning" or "application") is something most every law school graduate knows how to do. But writing that analysis down on paper (or "showing all of your work") is often problematic on the time-pressured bar exam.

What makes for a well-written analysis? Answer: **matching up specific facts to specific parts of the rule.** For most subjects, the integrated fact-rule format outlined in Chapter 2 will work well. As a general rule of thumb, break the rule into its separate parts and then apply the relevant fact(s) to show whether that part of the rule is or is not met—and do so in the same sentence to ensure you are matching facts to rules.

If there are two parts of the rule, there needs to be (at least) two sentences of application (again—application is matching up the relevant fact with the relevant part of the rule), and then a conclusion sentence. Here is a skeletal template (without reference to a specific situation) for writing out your essays:

> **Here** (element/rule part 1) is met **because** (fact A).
> **Also,** (element/rule part 2) is met **because** (fact B).
> **Finally,** (element/rule part 3) is met **because** (fact C).
> **Thus,** (the rule is satisfied).

If there is a valid counterargument to make, you can simply add "However (element/rule part 1) may not be met because (fact A)" to the format and note the counterargument. Admittedly, this format works better for some subjects than others. But regardless of subject, you still have different parts of rules—and you need to analyze each part of the rule by applying specific facts to specific parts of the rule. Regardless of whether you use this "template" or not, think of each essay issue you write out as its own "mini-essay" and be sure to apply facts to each part of the rule.

There is an art and a science
to everything in this world. In all things, learn technique,
but also tune in to the art behind the technique,
for that is what separates "good" from "great."

Good news—it's time to chop more wood. ☺ Below is a somewhat typical fact pattern that you might see on an essay exam. Read over the fact pattern carefully (but don't forget what you've already learned—read the call of the question first to ground yourself in the subject matter).

Example 3-1
Sample Fact Pattern—Criminal Law Essay

Sam was a petty thief who needed a big score. He heard that Old Man Bill Johnson had just purchased a $10,000 painting, which Sam thought he could easily sell to his art collector cousin. So Sam spent weeks staking out the Johnson house, "casing it" for the perfect crime. When Sam had the household routine down cold, he put his elaborate plan into action. One day, after Mr. Johnson left for work, Sam drove his car from down the street and parked in front of the Johnson house—which was no easy task because Sam had been drinking for several hours. Sam then ran to the Johnson's front door, kicked in the door, ran into the living room, and grabbed the $10,000 painting off of the wall. As Sam ran out of the house, he was startled to see Mr. Johnson standing in front of him in the driveway. Both men froze, but then Sam decided to make the best of the situation. "I need some meal money, pops," Sam yelled. "Give me your wallet or I'll bash your head in!" Mr. Johnson pulled out his cell phone and frantically started to dial." Sam kicked Mr. Johnson in the stomach, then pushed him to the ground. As Mr. Johnson wallowed on the ground in pain, Sam rifled through the elderly man's pants pockets. When Sam found the old man's wallet, he grabbed it, grabbed the painting and took off running. Old Man Bill Johnson suffered internal bleeding, and later died in surgery due to surgeon error.
Discuss and evaluate all crimes Sam may have committed, including any defenses.

If you read the call of the question first, you would immediately know that this was a Criminal Law essay. Hopefully, a few of the big issues jumped out at you right away. Let's discuss two of the big ones and look at some sample answers.

Burglary and robbery were two of the big issues that might have jumped out at you as you read the fact pattern. Here are the most commonly stated rules for both of those crimes:

Burglary: Breaking and entering into the dwelling of another with intent to commit a felony therein.

Robbery: Taking of property from the person of another by force or threat with intent to permanently deprive him of the property.

Keeping in mind the need for good fact application, take a look at the following sample answers for these two issues. Please note that the "model" answer is only a partial answer. There would certainly be other "issues" to address, but we are only going to discuss the issues of burglary and robbery.

Example 3-2

Partial "Model" Answer—Criminal Law Essay

<u>The first issue is, did the Defendant commit burglary?</u>
Burglary is defined as "breaking and entering into a dwelling of another with intent to commit a felony therein." Based on the facts given to us, Sam needed a big "score" so he kicked down the door of the Johnson house, walked inside and stole the $10,000 painting. As such, Sam is guilty of the crime of burglary.

<u>The second issue is, did the Defendant commit robbery?</u>
Robbery is defined as the "taking of property from the person of another by force or intimidation with intent to deprive him of it permanently." In the case at bar, after Sam left the house, he saw Mr. Johnson in front of him and yelled, "give me your wallet or I'll bash your head in." He then kicked Mr. Johnson in the stomach, pushed him to the ground, seized his wallet, and ran off with it. Thus, Sam has satisfied all of the elements of robbery and will be guilty of robbery.

So let's discuss the partial answer, starting with the burglary issue. Clearly, burglary is an issue—which is noted by the heading. The answer then identifies the correct rule with specificity. The answer then gives all of the relevant facts and a specific (and correct) conclusion. Perfect answer, right?

Not exactly. What's wrong with the answer? The IRAC format is followed perfectly, right? The issue is correctly identified, right? The correct rule is given, right? The answer then notes all of the relevant facts that bear on the relevant elements of burglary, right?

The last question is the relevant one. Yes, the answer does "note" all of the relevant facts, but there is no **application**—no actual analysis in the answer. The answer merely recites facts, which, as we now know, is not analysis. Again, you want to apply (e.g., link up) relevant facts with relevant parts of the rule. Stating the issue, stating the rule, listing facts, and coming up with the conclusion is a format many students "think" provides analysis, but it does not. Analysis is APPLYING facts to rules; reciting facts is not the same as applying facts.

Many students go through the analysis in their heads without correctly noting it on paper. Even though you think something is obvious, you must state the obvious to maximize your score. And I'll tell you how to be more effective at that in just a second. But first, let's take a look at the robbery answer, reprinted below:

The second issue is, did the Defendant commit robbery? Robbery is defined as the "taking of property from the person of another by force or intimidation with intent to deprive him of it permanently." In the case at bar, after Sam left the house, he saw Mr. Johnson in front of him and yelled, "give me your wallet or I'll bash your head in." He then kicked Mr. Johnson in the stomach, pushed him to the ground, seized his wallet, and ran off with it. Thus, Sam has satisfied all of the elements of robbery and will be guilty of robbery.

This answer has the same blueprint as the burglary answer, correct? At first glance, this seems like a very good answer—but, again, there is no actual analysis here. The writer is most likely going through the analysis in her head, but that is not what shows up on paper. And the grader can only give points for what is on paper.

So—how do we do a better job at giving our analysis or our "application?" In essence, show all of your work. Think of this like 8th grade math, and show all of your work to maximize your score. Even if it's obvious from the facts that a particular element or part of the rule is met, state which specific fact (or facts) makes it so. Don't recite facts, integrate facts—this is analysis. SHOW ALL OF YOUR WORK.

As a general rule of thumb, you want to break the rule into its separate parts. If there are two parts of the rule, there needs to be (at least) two sentences of application, and then a conclusion sentence. The format literally forces you to apply facts to parts of the rule, rather than recite facts and go through the analysis in your head.

Given our new format, how would we re-write our criminal essay dealing with Sam, Mr. Johnson, and the issues of burglary and robbery? At this point, if you really want to get the most out of this book, take a few minutes and try to write out an answer for both issues. (Feel free to refer back to the preceding pages for the applicable rules of law.)

Remember—practice is the key to doing well—especially when learning a new technique. And there is never any time better than the present moment to practice—practice writing the essay, practice being wholly present. You are preparing yourself for the day of the exam. Make the decision now that you will not take shortcuts on your path....

Make everything
your meditation.
Let the day become a moving meditation,
and make every moment wholly conscious.

☯   ☯   ☯

Before we look at a model answer, I'd like to throw out this disclaimer: **there are a number of ways** that you can write out an answer to our issues and get the full point value. The format I am suggesting is one that forces you to apply/analyze, and it should increase your overall efficiency. Thus, it works well, but other "blueprints" could work, too. Okay ... let's look at these answers, starting with burglary. I have given the "old" answer and the "new" together for a basis of comparison.

Example 3-3
The "Old" Burglary Answer

<u>The first issue is, did the Defendant commit burglary?</u>
Burglary is defined as "breaking and entering into a dwelling of another with intent to commit a felony therein." Based on the facts given to us, it is clear that Sam needed a big "score" so he kicked down the door of the Johnson house. Sam then walked inside of the Johnson house and took the $10,000 painting off of the Johnson's wall. As such, Sam is guilty of the crime of burglary.

The "New" Burglary Answer

<u>Burglary</u>
Burglary is defined as "breaking and entering into a dwelling of another with intent to commit a felony therein." Here, Sam committed breaking and entering because he kicked down the door and entered the house. Also, it was a dwelling of another because Mr. Johnson lived there. Furthermore, Sam had the requisite intent to commit theft because he had been "casing the place" for weeks and was going to "sell" the painting to his art collector cousin. Finally, he committed theft because he took Mr. Johnson's $10,000 painting from inside the house. Thus, Sam is guilty of burglary.

The first difference you will notice is that you do not have to write out, "The issue is whether Defendant is guilty of burglary" or whatever crime you are discussing. It's sufficient just to give the issue its own heading, as I've done in the "new" answer. Every little bit of time you save might come into play on the last essay.

Of course, after noting the issue you are discussing, the applicable rule needs to be the first thing you write down. And in our example, it is. There are no wasted words to introduce it—it just states the applicable rule with specificity.

Note how each part of the rule is matched up with a specific fact or facts that prove to the grader exactly how and why each part of the rule is met. Also note how the question provides all of the facts you need to match up to all parts of the rule. Now let's take a look at the two robbery answers—the "old" one and the "new" one.

Example 3-4
The "Old" Robbery Answer

The second issue is, did the Defendant commit robbery?
Robbery is defined as the "taking of property from the person of another by force or intimidation with intent to deprive him of it permanently." In the case at bar, after Sam left the house, he saw Mr. Johnson in front of him and yelled, "give me your wallet or I'll bash your head in." He then kicked Mr. Johnson in the stomach, pushed him to the ground, seized his wallet, and ran off with it. Thus, Sam has satisfied all of the elements of robbery and will be guilty of robbery.

The "New" Robbery Answer

Robbery
Robbery is the "taking of property from the person of another by force or intimidation with intent to deprive him of it permanently." Here, Sam took property from the person of Mr. Johnson because Sam rifled through the victim's pockets and took his wallet. Also, he did so by force because he kicked the victim in the stomach and pushed him to the ground. Finally, he did so with intent to permanently

deprive the victim of his wallet, as evidenced by him saying, "I need meal money." Thus, Sam satisfies all of the elements of robbery and will be guilty of robbery.

Note again how the "old" answer does indeed list the relevant facts. The facts, however, are merely listed and not integrated into an analysis. Here's a rule of thumb: never list a fact unless it is within a sentence that proves or negates part of the rule. Also note how often the word "because" appears in the "new" answers. The word "because" is an analysis word and should show up throughout your essays. (For additional examples of writing in a manner that "shows all of your work," see Appendix C.)

At this point, some of you might be thinking—this format is far too simplistic for a bar exam analysis. But in the Zen mind, simple is profound. Moreover, you want to keep your essay writing simple because you are going to be in a serious time crunch. And, finally, you want to keep it simple because that usually makes for a better read—one that will make your grader happy. The graders have their grading rubric of issues, rules, and points of analyses (e.g., key facts upon which each analysis turns) that they are looking for, and the easier you make it for them to read, the better your score is going to be.

You have a challenging task ahead of you. You have a LOT of law to learn in a relatively short amount of time. You want to go into the exam with a specific plan as to how you are going to write your essays. With practice, your format or "template" should be second-nature to you. It doesn't have to be the format I am suggesting, but it needs to be a format where you are integrating fact and law in your writing. Keep chopping wood.

A story is told of two monks
who had taken a vow to never touch a woman.
They're on a pilgrimage to a holy temple when they come to a
Place where the water has risen, making it difficult to pass.
Stranded along the bank is a beautiful young lady who asks
for their help. The first monk scowls at her and says that he's

taken a vow of chastity, so he cannot help her. The second picks the woman up and carries her silently across the water. A mile later, the first monk asks the second, "What did you do? You know that we're not allowed to touch women — why did you take her across the river?"

The second monk answers, "Brother, I picked her up, carried her across the river, and set her down. You've been carrying her for the past mile."

Along your journey, you are sure to experience times where you deviate from your path. Perhaps you deviate from your study schedule or blow off going to a bar review lecture. It's bound to happen, so don't beat yourself up — live in the present, not the past. Let go of any negative thoughts — they will not serve you.

Similarly, there are bound to be practice essays you "bomb" or don't do as well as you would have liked. Move on — let it go. This is inevitable and will happen to everyone. And, if this happens on the actual exam, then this piece of advice is even more important. Dwelling on how poorly (or even how well) you did on a previous essay will only detract from your focus on the essay you are currently writing.

You should know going into the exam that there will likely be an essay question or two that throws you for a loop. It happens to everyone. Answer the best you can, and LET IT GO. Of course, the more you have practiced being "present" in all that you do, the easier it will be to let go of a prior essay.

A Quick Recap on Essay Writing: The Least You Need to Know About Writing Your Analyses

- You do NOT get any credit for merely listing facts.
- You don't get very many points for merely listing conclusions.
- My rule of thumb: never list a fact unless you are "analyzing" it—which means integrating facts with rules.
- Don't *list* facts; *integrate* facts into the analysis.
- Match up specific facts with specific parts of the rule that govern the issue you are discussing.
- If the fact pattern quotes someone's words, those words are important; most of the time you will want to quote them back in your analysis.
- You have to state the obvious to get credit for knowing the obvious.
- Show all of your work!
- After you are done answering a question, let it go.
- Be Simple.
- Be Present.
- Stay Positive.
- Pass the Bar Exam.

4. Noreuil's Top Ten Tips for Essay Writing

*Live life
in the present.
This moment is the
only thing that's real;
worrying about the future
and lamenting the past only
crowds out the beauty of
what is happening now.*

The beauty of what is happening now is that after tutoring for many years, I am going to share with you the top ten tips I have learned for doing well on essay exams. Be present—and enjoy.

(1) Before the Exam, Know the "Big Ticket" Topics

By looking at past exams you should have a good idea as to what subjects are most often tested. Know these going into the exam, and devote practice time to these topics. On a similar note, it is rare that "lesser-tested" topics will be tested on back-to-back exams. I am not, however, in any way, shape, or form suggesting that you should ignore topics that were tested on your state's most recent bar exam. But, at the same time, it's good to be aware of patterns of subjects tested.

(2) Have a Template for Writing Out the "Big Ticket" Issues

We have talked about a template for writing your answers. You certainly don't have to use mine, but have something in mind before going into the test. With the time pressures you will be under, you want to be sure you know exactly how you are going to write out your answers. The template I have discussed up to this point has been more of a template for writing your analyses. But you should also have a template for writing out the often tested (or "big ticket") issues, which have many nuances to them. In this regard, think of a template as a flow chart for how you are going to answer an issue.

For example, in an open-ended Contracts question your template might address: contract formation (offer, acceptance, consideration); breach of the contract (seller breach, buyer breach); available remedies; and then damages (consequential, compensatory, etc.). Of course, within each applicable sub-issue you would want to be sure to write out a sound application applying fact to law.

Another example of a template flow chart might be from search and seizure in a criminal procedure essay. Your flow chart might chronologically address whether there was: governmental conduct; a reasonable expectation of privacy; a valid police warrant; an exception to the warrant requirement (consent, plain view, exigent circumstances, etc.).

(3) Be Definitive When Giving Conclusions

Be conscious of being definitive when giving your ultimate conclusions. Over the course of my years of tutoring, I have seen too many "wishy-washy" conclusions—all of which leave the grader unhappy. My all-time "favorite" wishy-washy answer (which sadly I've seen on several occasions from those I've tutored): "John will win if a judge or jury finds in his favor." Obviously, you want to be a little (okay, a LOT) more definitive than this to keep your grader happy.

Be as definitive as you can be—even if you're unsure of the correct conclusion. Try to avoid using words such as "may" or "possibly" in your final conclusion. Here are a few examples to try to avoid:

Thus, the evidence may be admissible.

Thus, it's possible that John might win a negligence claim against Bill.

Thus, John may have committed the crime of arson.

Thus, it's arguable that the will is valid.

Bar exam essays almost always have a "correct" conclusion. Be definitive to be most effective. Sometimes, an examinee is reluctant to be definitive because he isn't sure of the conclusion. If this is the case, use your best judgment and pick an outcome. The words "likely" or "unlikely" are effective modifiers. Below are rewrites of the above "wishy-washy" examples:

Thus, the evidence is likely admissible.

Thus, it's unlikely that John will win a negligence claim against Bill.

Thus, John likely committed the crime of arson.

Thus, it's likely that the will is valid.

Note that you can get substantial credit for the wrong conclusion—this is where the "analysis" comes into play. In fact, here is a quote from the National Conference of Bar Examiners:

> "Appropriate credit is given in the grading of essay answers for well reasoned analyses of the issues and legal principles involved even though the final conclusion itself may be incorrect."

Again—well reasoned analyses are those that APPLY facts to law (e.g., the format I outlined in previous chapters). If your analyses flow well, you can still get substantial credit for the wrong conclusion—so be definitive and confident.

(4) Try to Sound Like a Lawyer

You are going through this exam to be admitted to the practice of law—so try to sound like a lawyer whenever possible. Use verbs that lawyers use. For example, don't write that the court should *reject* the petition; write that the court should *dismiss* the petition. Similarly, you don't want to write that the prosecutor's objection should be *denied*, you want to write that it should be *overruled*. A judge doesn't *overrule* a default judgment, a judge *vacates* a default judgment. A police officer doesn't *take* drugs; an officer *seizes* drugs. A Plaintiff doesn't "lose" or "forgo" a potential defense by not pleading it at the right time; a Plaintiff "waives" such a defense.

In a similar vein, be sure to use "terms of art" to sound more "lawyer-like." For example, on an Evidence question, don't write that a statement was a "contradictory statement" to what the defendant said earlier; write that it was a "prior inconsistent statement." On a Wills question, if you are discussing a child who was born after the execution of the deceased's will, refer to the child by her legal moniker—a pretermitted child. You are getting ready to be a lawyer—so be sure you sound like one on the bar exam.

(5) Look for Verbal Clues in the Fact Pattern

Look for verbal clues that will give rise to issues—because they are often present in the fact patterns. For example, if the word "precluded" is used in a Civil Procedure question, that might mean collateral estoppel comes into play. If the phrase "relied upon" is used in a Contracts question, that might be begging for a promissory estoppel analysis.

Additionally, if the word "admitted" is used to describe what one party to a lawsuit said in evidence, think about party admissions or statements against interest under the rules for hearsay exceptions. If someone "orally agrees" to a contract, you might be looking at a statute of frauds issue. If a statute is involved in a Torts question, think about negligence per se. Every fact usually matters—so read critically.

Moreover, pay close attention to ages (especially in a Contracts question, because a minor cannot legally enter into a contract with a merchant) and specific dates. Also, look for words that comprise part of the law—e.g., someone acting "mistakenly" or "unreasonably" or "without authority."

(6) Answer the Specific Question Asked

This is something mentioned earlier that deserves elaboration—because it happens so often on bar exams. Don't waste time trying to impress the graders with all of the esoteric and arcane information you know about a particular subject. You will NOT get credit for gratuitously added information—no matter how esoteric the information is. ANSWER THE SPECIFIC QUESTION ASKED.

I often see examinees giving what I refer to as a "brain dump" on certain essay answers. A "brain dump" is exactly what you think—dumping a bunch of rules that aren't relevant to the question. Resist this temptation. It is better to write nothing and move on to the next subject (as opposed to writing about the evolution of a particular legal rule). Remember—time is at a premium. Don't use the last ten minutes of a civil procedure question to brain dump when that time could be more wisely spent on the next essay(s).

(7) Answer Sub-Questions in the Order They Are Presented

Within a particular subject, the call of the question may ask several specific questions. (Evidence questions, in particular, break up the overall "question" into subparts.) If so, answer them in the order they were asked. The graders' "grading rubric" will be in the same order as the enumerated sub-questions, so that's the way you should answer them. Below is an example from the July 2004 Arizona Bar Exam (Contracts). The call of the question is stated as follows:

1. Is there a valid contract, and if so, what are its terms?
2. If a valid contract exists, is either side in breach? Explain your answer.
3. What, if any, remedies are available to the parties?

In the above example, you would want to answer the questions in the same order they were presented. You might feel better (e.g., more knowledgeable) about responding to the "remedies" part of the question, but resist the temptation. Your goal is to make the grader happy.

Again, you may be tempted to answer the second part of the question first—perhaps because you "know it" better. Regardless, answer in the order the call of the question outlines. The above examples may appear obvious as to the order in which you would write out your answer, but other questions may be much more tempting to answer "out of order."

(8) Short-Cuts

A) Repeating Rules

On the time-pressured bar exam, you oftentimes need a short-cut. If you have occasion to repeat a rule that governs a particular issue, you can just write "See Rule Above." Of course, if you type your answer, you can just copy and paste. Repeating rules often comes into play in evidence, where you may have to give the rule for relevance three times when discussing three different pieces of evidence. Regardless of typing or writing, if you repeat rules, **be sure to give the application to that rule for each issue.** It's not enough just to say "See Rule Above" if you don't have any application.

B) Use a Short-Cut for Rule Explanations

If time becomes an issue (and it often does), you might have to use short-cuts during certain essays. The best place to do this is during your "rule explanations." Oftentimes a rule of law will contain a word or phrase that needs to be defined (also known as a "rule explanation" or a "rule within a rule"). If this happens, and you are running short on time, a parenthetical explanation defining the word or phrase might be your best bet. Of course, in an ideal world, you won't have time constraints and won't need to take any short-cuts, but the bar exam doesn't take place in the ideal world.

Below are two examples. The first is a standard "rule" and applicable "rule explanation" for first-degree murder. Note how the second example takes a "short-cut" with the explanation of malice aforethought.

Example 4-1 (from Criminal law)

First-degree murder is the unjustified killing of another with malice aforethought and causation. Malice aforethought means acting purposefully or knowingly.

Example 4-2 (from Criminal law)

First-degree murder is the unjustified killing of another with malice aforethought (acting purposefully and knowingly) and causation.

The second example is from Contracts. We all know that the "rule" for contract formation requires a valid offer, acceptance, and consideration. Sometimes, however, the "rule explanation" of one or more of those terms is critical to analyzing the problem. Example 4-3 shows a standard rule and rule explanation, while Example 4-4 illustrates the rule explanation short-cuts.

Example 4-3 (from Contracts)

A contract requires offer, acceptance, and consideration. An offer is a promise containing specific and definite terms. Acceptance must be unequivocal and mirror the terms of the offer. Consideration is a bargained for exchange.

Example 4-4 (from Contracts)

A contract requires offer (a promise of specific and definite terms), acceptance (unequivocally mirroring the terms of the offer), and consideration (a bargained for exchange).

Again, I would only suggest using this type of short-cut if you are pressed for time. The "short-cut" I propose here won't save you twenty minutes, but it might save you enough time at the end to write out one more issue, or one more application—which might just get you the additional point or two you need to pass.

(9) Use Transition Words (or "Signposts")

One of your goals is to make each essay appear professional and easy to read. First, use headings for your issues to guide the reader. Within each issue, use transition words whenever you can. A few examples: Also, Furthermore, Moreover, Additionally, Although, Conversely, However, Therefore, and Thus. And don't be afraid to use the generic, "First … Second … Next …" transitions. Write simply: the easier you make it on the grader to understand and follow, the better off you will be.

(10) After You Answer a Question, LET IT GO

This may be number ten on the list, but I cannot overstate how important it is to be focused during the exam—practice being present at all times. Once you have answered a question, let it go and move on. Thinking about how poorly (or even how well) you did on a previous essay will only detract from your focus.

Be present at every moment of the bar exam—don't think about past questions or future questions. Stay in the moment as often as you can, and if you find your mind drifting to the past or the future, let the thought go and bring your attention back to the present.

What the Graders Say

A recent survey of bar essay graders conducted by the NCBE found that the single biggest mistake examinees make is not responding to the specific call of the question. This just reinforces the importance of reading the call of the question first—and then again before you start writing. Remember—don't just "brain dump" all you know about a particular subject or issue; answer the specific call of the question, and if you don't know how to answer, move on to the next question.

5. Studying for the Multi State Bar Exam

Zen demands intelligence and will power,
as do all the greater things we desire to become real.
— Carl Jung

Similar to practicing essay writing, you are also given the great privilege of chopping wood for the Multistate Bar Examination ("MBE"). The MBE is an objective six-hour examination containing 200 multiple choice questions. The examination is divided into two sessions of three hours each, one in the morning and one in the afternoon, with 100 questions in each period. Each state varies as to the weight given to the MBE and the essay portions of the bar exam.

The examination includes questions in the following areas: Constitutional Law, Contracts, Criminal Law and Procedure, Evidence, Real Property, and Torts. There are 34 questions each in Contracts and Torts and 33 questions each in Constitutional Law, Criminal Law and Procedure, Evidence, and Real Property.

So ... what exactly is tested under each of the seven major subjects? The National Conference of Bar Examiner's website provides you with topic (and sub-topic) coverage for each subject. The website address is www.ncbex.org. If you click on "MBE" on the left-hand side, it will bring you to the MBE page and you can click on subject matter outlines. These outlines cover everything that could be tested per subject.

Moreover, the outlines give you the percentile breakdown of what's covered per subject. For example, the topic of negligence comprises approximately 50% of the 34 Torts MBE questions. For Contracts, approximately 25% of the questions are UCC questions. I encourage you to check it out and get a feel for which topics are more commonly tested than others.

How to Study for the MBE

Everything I have said about the parallel of the practice of Zen and practice of essay writing applies to studying for the MBE as well. I won't repeat the parallels here, but suffice it to say that awareness, focus, balance, discipline, perspective, and practice are again essential to achieving your ultimate goal.

Above all, you have to know the law to do well on the MBE. Knowing the law is the first step to doing well on the MBE, but it is by no means the only step. The questions on the MBE are designed to test your ability to critically analyze a fact pattern vis-à-vis the applicable law. Accordingly, knowing how to study for the MBE is critical to your success.

First—do practice questions. Do as many as you can. You can get questions (and annotated answers) from your bar review course, and from the National Conference of Bar Examiners. The bar examiners will often release old MBE questions. Additionally, you can pay $26 for a sample of 100 MBE questions (with annotated answers) that are actually written by the same people who write the MBE questions. To do this, go to http://www.ncbex.org/mbe-ap.

You want to spend a lot of your study time doing practice questions. But "doing" practice questions cannot be a means to an end. You cannot just "do" 34 questions, check the answers and be done. This is one of those times when quality really does win out over quantity. It is important to know why the correct answer choice is correct—but it is equally (if not more) important to know why the incorrect answers are wrong.

For every question that you do, read each annotated answer and see not only why the correct answer is correct, but **why the incorrect answers are incorrect**. I cannot stress this enough (which is why I repeated it from above). Why is this important? It's important because when you understand why answers are incorrect, you start to see patterns emerging as to how some answers can throw you off.

The MBE, like all multiple choice tests, often comes down to a process of elimination. In fact, sometimes you will pick an answer not because you know that it is correct, but because you know the other three answers are NOT correct. And once you are familiar with why wrong answers are wrong, they are much easier to eliminate.

When the task is done beforehand, then it is easy.
— *Zen master Yuan-tong*

Starting the MBE Study Process

Your goal is to have so much familiarity with the law and the various types of multiple choice questions, that, on the day of the exam, your preparation will have (virtually) made your task completed beforehand. This can only happen if you practice diligently and correctly. Here are my recommendations....

At first, I recommend practicing one subject at a time. If you divide your MBE sessions into a certain number of questions, do all of the questions from the subject that you have been studying that day. Immersing yourself in a subject can help make connections between interrelated concepts, as well as reinforce learning and memorization.

Before you begin any practice session, I would suggest taking time to go over your outline on that particular subject to get in the right frame of mind. If it's Torts day, get in the Torts frame of mind.

I also suggest keeping an MBE log for each subject. Write down the number correct every time you do practice questions for each subject. See what your percentage is for each subject, and see what subjects are a strength for you and which are a weakness. Generally speaking, the target percentage you want to hit is somewhere around sixty-five percent (65%).

Also, take note if there is a particular sub-issue within each subject that you are continuing to miss. If you can identify that the UCC questions are difficult for you, maybe that is a sign to get some additional study aids on that sub-issue. Or maybe you are always missing questions on custodial interrogation in Criminal Procedure. Awareness is key — you are probably not going to be great in every subject, but identifying your weaknesses is the first step to overcoming them.

Of course, as time draws closer to exam day, it will be a good idea to answer questions in a random fashion because that's how they will come at you on the exam. In fact, I would recommend doing a simulated exam at least once. A "simulated" exam would be in the same format as the bar — 100 questions in a mock morning session and 100 questions in an afternoon session (with all the question subjects in random order).

Timing

If you break down the timing of the exam, you have to finish 100 questions in three (3) hours—which equates to 1.8 minutes per question. This translates to about 34 questions per hour. Thus, I suggest doing one-hour sessions of a particular subject when you are ready to start answering questions.

If you need to build your way up to it (or don't have the time for an hour session), you can do 17 questions in thirty minutes. But remember—part of the process is conditioning yourself (both mentally and physically) to be able to do two three-hour sessions of 100 questions each. Accordingly, if you can do one-hour sessions of 34 questions, it will better prepare you for the marathon of game day. Moreover, it will give you a more accurate indication as to how you are doing with timing.

Whenever you do an MBE session, always take note of your time. Write down your start time and your finish time. Are you within the time you need to be? If not, are you improving on your timing the more you practice? Again—awareness is key. And you cannot be aware if you don't take note of your time. To get an accurate gauge of your timing, be very strict about doing practice questions under test conditions (no phone, no TV, etc.).

On the day of the exam, it's a good idea to know exactly where you are in regard to your remaining time. If you use the formula noted above (34 questions per hour), you can write out your "time markers" before you read the first question. For example, if you begin the exam at 9:10, you can quickly write out the following:

Time	Question #
9:40	17
10:10	33
10:40	50
11:10	67
11:40	84
12:10	100

Being aware of exactly where you are during the three-hour marathon will help when you are taking the exam. Of course, in an ideal world, your practice sessions will give you a good idea as to whether time will or will not be an issue the day of the exam. You don't want to spend an inordinate amount of time on any one question—they are all worth the same amount of points. If you get bogged down on a question, you probably have no better chance of getting the correct answer if you spend two minutes on it or twenty. If a question is that difficult, answer it and move on.

Do note, however, that no matter how much you practice, it will be difficult to simulate the conditions and emotions you are feeling while taking the actual exam. As such, just because you have always been "on time" during your practice sessions, that doesn't necessarily mean your time will be the same on exam day. Be safe and track your time.

Great Faith. Great Doubt. Great Effort.
— The three qualities necessary for training.

Reviewing Your Practice MBE Questions

I cannot stress enough the importance of putting in the effort to review each of your MBE questions—even the ones you answered correctly. After each session, as you "grade" (or "review") all of the annotated answers—try to figure out WHY you missed a particular question. Consider:

1. Did you miss it because you didn't know the law?

2. Did you overlook an important fact?

3. Did you confuse the parties?

4. Did you fail to recognize the rule that governs the issue?

5. Did you misapply the facts to the rule?

6. Did you mischaracterize a fact or assume a fact not specifically noted?

7. Did you have a problem focusing?

8. Did you misread the call of the question?

Again — knowing yourself is critical to reaching your ultimate goal, and you can only truly know yourself if you ask some of the questions above. If the problem was your focus, was it because it was late in the day or was it because you have a mental block with that particular subject (which could be due to an evil law school professor or poor grade, etc.)?

Regardless of the reason you missed a particular question, the more you realize **why** you are getting questions wrong, the better chance you have to fix it. And that's what's great about annotated answers — they help you to see where you go awry.

When you grade or review the answers, see why answers are right, see why answers are wrong, look for patterns, figure out why you are missing the ones that you do, and gauge your time. And remember — even if you get a question right, you should still check to see why all of the other answers are wrong.

As a final comment on preparation, if at all possible, try to study at the same time every day — preferably the same times you will be taking the exam. Again, it's a marathon, not a sprint, and you are conditioning your brain, so condition it to be focused at the same times that you will be taking the actual exam whenever possible.

Breaking Down the MBE

At its core, the MBE is really a reading comprehension test. You have to understand and digest the fact pattern. Second, you have to know the applicable law. But that's just the start.

The real key to the MBE is being able to apply the substantive law to the fact pattern in order to pick the best answer. This "art" is often referred to as logical reasoning, and it is usually the most difficult part of the MBE. There is one "most correct" answer, and there are usually other "plausible, but not as correct" answers. Again, this is not a test geared toward rote memorization of the law. The application of law to fact is critical.

As you all probably know, you will be given a fact pattern, then asked a specific question, then asked to choose the most correct answer out of four. What you are asked—or the "Call of the Question"—can take various forms, largely depending on the particular subject being tested. Here are a few examples:

a. What is the Plaintiff's most likely theory of recovery?

b. What is the Defendant's best defense to the charges?

c. Does A have a cause of action against B?

d. How should the judge rule on the prosecutor's objection?

e. Which of the following is the most likely outcome in A's suit against B?

Practice will give you intimate familiarity with the various calls of the question, but you probably get the picture from the above examples. Now that you have the context for this portion of the exam, let's dive into some MBE strategies for maximizing your score.

Read the Call of the Question First

Similar to essays, you should read the call of the question first. The call will usually only be a sentence or two, and reading it first won't markedly add to your overall time. There are several reasons to read the call of the question before you read the fact pattern.

First, knowing exactly what is being asked is crucial. Similar to essay writing, reading the call of the question first will help ground you in the subject matter, so you can get into a Contracts frame of mind when you are reading the question. When you practice, most of the time you will practice a particular subject (such as "Torts"). As such, you are already in a "Torts frame of mind" for each question of that practice session.

Remember that, similar to essay questions, the MBE questions come at you randomly and sometimes you won't be sure whether you are reading a Contracts, Property, or Torts question until you get to the call of the question. If, however, you read the call of the question first, you will know what subject is being tested and can approach the facts with that topic in mind (similar to how you practiced).

Reading the call of the question first gives you context as you begin reading the fact pattern. Different facts may take on a different significance for different subjects, depending on exactly what is being asked. As such, the call of the question may help you know exactly what you are looking for in the fact pattern, thereby saving you time.

To illustrate the latter point, sometimes a question will specifically ask you to adopt a particular side's viewpoint—in which case you will want to read the facts with a certain party's interests in mind. Usually (but not always), these types of questions will ask for a party's "best argument." Here are a few examples of what I'm talking about from actual released questions. (I have only listed the calls of the questions and not the entire fact patterns.)

> His best argument for being found NOT guilty is that he ...

> The strongest constitutional argument to support Owner's claim is ...

> If A sues B for breach of contract, which of the following facts, if established, would most strengthen A's case?

> The strongest ground upon which A could challenge the regulation is that it violates the ...

> If B wins, it will be because ...

As you can see, there are many types of these "best argument" questions. Obviously, it's helpful to know what party you are going to make an argument for before you read the facts, so reading the call of the question is particularly invaluable for these types of questions. Moreover, you can also see that the "call" is often just a single sentence, which shouldn't eat up too much of your time.

The quieter you become,
the more you are able to hear.

Critical Reading — the Fact Pattern

After you have read the call of the question, read the fact pattern *critically*. Reading critically is all about being fully present in each moment. After you have read the fact pattern, be sure to re-read the call of the question. A common mistake test takers make is to get in such a hurry that they actually misread what is being asked in the call of the question. If you are going to be sure of anything, be sure of *exactly* what is being asked. READING CAREFULLY is key, and reading the call of the question is the biggest part of this key.

After you have read the call of the question and then read the fact pattern, the next thing you should do is look for the issue. Yes — contrary to what you may believe — issue spotting plays a significant role on the MBE. Remember — issues always come from facts, and after a lot of practice, you will be able to spot the main issue in many MBE questions.

Once you know the issue, think about the rule that governs that issue. By knowing exactly what the issue is, and the rule that governs it, you can often eliminate a response or two. This is because often an incorrect answer will give a correct legal rule to an inapplicable legal theory (e.g., one that does not govern the issue at hand).

For example, if the "issue" is negligence, and one of the answers gives the rule for *res ipsa loquitor*, that answer choice can be eliminated. If, for example, the "issue" is strict liability, and one of the answer choices talked about the "rule" for negligence, then that answer will be incorrect. Remember — just because an answer choice correctly states a legal rule, that doesn't mean it's the best answer for that particular question.

Let's take a look at a few questions to illustrate what I'm saying. The following examples are from past MBE questions that have been released by the NCBE.

MBE SAMPLE QUESTION #1[9]

Chemco manufactured a liquid chemical product known as XRX. Some XRX leaked from a storage tank on Chemco's property, seeped into the groundwater, flowed to Farmer's adjacent property, and polluted Farmer's well. Several of Farmer's cows drank the polluted well water and died. If Farmer brings an action against Chemco to recover the value of the cows that died, Farmer will

A) prevail, because a manufacturer is strictly liable for harm caused by its products.

B) prevail, because the XRX escaped from Chemco's premises.

C) not prevail, unless farmer can establish that the storage tank was defective.

D) not prevail, unless Chemco failed to exercise reasonable care in storing the XRX.

Using our "Issue-spot first" method, we identify the issue first. Here, the issue is strict liability (specifically, a possessor-of-land's strict liability). Then we think about the rule for strict liability and we can easily eliminate answer choices C and D because they both deal with the rule for negligence. Answer C implicitly does so and D overtly does so by giving part of the "rule" regarding negligence — by noting the "failure to exercise reasonable care."

So if you identify the issue first, you can often eliminate an answer or two that deals with a different legal theory or issue. Remember — ISSUES always come from FACTS. (And, in case you are wondering, B is the correct answer to MBE Sample Question #1.)

9. The sample MBE questions contained in this book are actual released questions and are copyrighted by the National Conference of Bar Examiners (NCBE) and reprinted herein with permission. No part of any question may be reproduced or transmitted in any form or by any means (including photocopying) unless expressly permitted in writing by the NCBE. The author greatly thanks the NCBE for this permission.

Moreover, if an answer choice states a rule from a different legal theory (e.g., a theory not at issue from the facts) then you can eliminate it. For example, if a fact pattern gives rise to a commerce clause issue, and an answer choice gives a rule that pertains to a different constitutional power, you know you can eliminate it. The key is to spot the issue and know the rule of law that governs it.

Let's look at another example, this one from Criminal Law:

MBE SAMPLE QUESTION #2

Despondent over losing his job, Wilmont drank all night at a bar. While driving home, he noticed a car following him and, in his intoxicated state, concluded he was being followed by robbers. In fact, a police car was following him on suspicion of drunk driving. In his effort to get away, Wilmont sped through a stop sign and struck and killed a pedestrian. He was arrested by the police.

Wilmont is prosecuted for manslaughter. He should be

A. acquitted, because he honestly believed he faced an imminent threat of death or severe bodily injury.

B. acquitted, because his intoxication prevented him from appreciating the risk he created.

C. convicted, because he acted recklessly and in fact was in no danger.

D. convicted, because he acted recklessly and his apprehension of danger was not reasonable.

In the question above, the overall issue is clearly stated in the call of the question: manslaughter. Answer A appears to give correct reasoning (Wilmont likely did have an honest belief that he faced an imminent threat of death or severe bodily injury because he thought he was being chased by robbers). The reasoning, however, pertains to the issue of self-defense, not manslaughter. Accordingly, Answer A can immediately be eliminated. (In case you are wondering, the correct answer is D.)

How do you become an adept MBE issue spotter? The same way you do with essay issue spotting: practice. You are chopping wood (perhaps as a labor of love?), but are you present when you are chopping? Be sure when you practice that you are focusing on the FACTS in order to decipher the specific issue.

Normally, we do not so much look
at things as overlook them.

Eliminating Answer Choices

No matter how much you study for the MBE, you will not know the answer to every question. Moreover, you will be forced to make an educated guess on some of the questions. Being able to eliminate answer choices is critical to doing well on the MBE. If you are diligent in preparing, you will become more adept at spotting the reasons why some answer choices are incorrect. Look for the patterns when reviewing answer choices. Here are a few of the big reasons why answer choices can be wrong (and therefore eliminated):

(1)   The answer mischaracterizes the facts.

(2)   The answer choice assumes a fact in dispute.

(3)   The answer's reasoning is legally incorrect.

(4)   The law is stated incorrectly.

(5)   The answer applies the minority rule (rather than the majority rule).

As to (5), it is important to know that if a question is silent as to which law to apply (the majority or minority rule), always apply the majority rule. Do note, however, that the MBE does in fact question you on minority rules. Just don't apply them unless you are told to do so in the question.

(6)   A rule of law is perfectly stated, but it is inapplicable to the issue raised by the facts.

I alluded to (6) when talking about issues and inapplicable rules of law, but I'd like to re-emphasize this point because it's an important one. Keep an eye out for a perfectly stated rule of law that doesn't apply to the given fact pattern. This type of "wrong" answer can really trip you up because you see a perfectly articulated and CORRECT rule of law, and you are looking for the CORRECT answer, so this must be the choice. But, hopefully, now that you are aware of it, you will look to identify an issue (when applicable) and not fall into this trap.

(7)   An answer choice can be wrong even if it's a "correct" answer.

The answer choice noted by (7) is a tough one. But it's true—an answer choice can still be "wrong" even if it's factually and legally correct. How could an answer be wrong if it's both legally and factually correct? Remember—we're not looking for a "right" answer, we're looking for the "best" answer. Accordingly, multiple answers could be "correct" but the "most correct" answer (among multiple correct answers) usually is "most correct" because it's more precise and/or contains more reasoning.

Always remember: you are looking for the MOST CORRECT or the BEST answer for that particular fact pattern. This means that **every part** of the answer must be correct for it to be a viable choice:

It must state the correct law;

It must correctly characterize the facts;

It must have sound application of law to fact—or to put it another way, it must have correct, logical legal reasoning;

And, finally, it (almost always) needs to address and resolve a central issue raised from the fact pattern.

Most of the time the correct answer is not going to jump out at you. The process of elimination is a crucial part of taking (and doing well on) the MBE. Knowing the primary reasons why answer choices can be eliminated will go far toward you passing the bar exam. Learn them, live them, love them.

☯ ☯ ☯

A Quick Recap on the MBE: The Least You Need to Know on Strategies for Answering MBE Questions

- Read the call of the question first.
- Read the fact pattern critically—the MBE is first and foremost a reading comprehension test.
- Even before you look at the answer choices, try to decide the issue.
- Once you know the issue, think about the rule that governs that issue (and, of course, any exceptions to that rule).
- Then, read the answer choices and try to eliminate as many choices as you can.
- Remember that for an answer choice to be correct, *every part of the answer* must be correct.
- When practicing MBE questions, always look at the annotated answers to see why answers are incorrect; look for patterns as to why answers are incorrect. This will help you with the process of elimination.
- After you are done answering a question, let it go.
- Be Simple.
- Be Present.
- Stay Positive.
- Pass the Bar Exam.

6. Noreuil's Top Ten Tips for the MBE

In the beginner's mind there are
many possibilities, in the expert's mind there are few.

(1) Don't Ever Assume Facts

Don't ever assume facts or read facts into the fact pattern if they aren't explicitly stated. Unlike law school exams, there are no "omitted facts" in the fact pattern. As such, you should never read into the question facts that are not there. Similarly, never assume any facts. A fact is either there in the fact pattern or it is not. Period.

(2) Assume That Every Fact Is Important

As a corollary to #1, always assume that every fact in every question is important ... because it usually is. Even facts that seem meaningless are more likely than not important. There are very few red herrings on bar exam essays. Accordingly, for the most part (not always, but for the most part), all given facts are important. So treat them as such when reading the fact patterns.

As you read the fact pattern, ask yourself: why might this fact be important? Of course, if you have read the call of the question first (which you will have done because you have read this book), you will have a much better context for figuring out why a particular fact might be important. And, as with the essay portion of the exam, pay particular attention to dates, ages, and dollar amounts. Also, be sure to take note of words that describe how a party is acting: intentionally, knowingly, unknowingly, mistakenly, unconsciously, reasonably, unreasonably, etc.

(3) Avoid Skipping Around from Question to Question

Answer the questions in the order they are presented. Skipping questions could result in your answers being mis-marked on the bubble sheet—and that is the worst possible thing that can happen on the MBE. Moreover, you likely won't have enough time to pick and choose your preferred subject questions first.

Answer each question in order, and if you have to guess before moving on, then guess, but perhaps put a star by that question so you can come back to it if you have time left over. Furthermore, be sure to answer every question because you do not lose points for incorrect answers.

(4) If Two Answers Are Opposite, One Is Probably True

This appears self-evident (and it is), but it brings up a larger point about "opposite answers" that I want to make. Most of the time answer choices will be split among outcomes, with two answers concluding one way and two answers concluding the opposite way. For example, two answer choices will conclude that A is guilty of the charged crime, and two answers that A is not guilty.

There are, however, times when the answer choices are split three-to-one, meaning three answers have one outcome and one answer concludes the opposite way. You may be duped into thinking that whenever this happens, the "correct" answer most likely comes from the group of three answers. Do not make this mistake. In fact, the opposite is often true—the stand alone conclusion is just as likely (if not more likely) to be correct than any of the other three. Here are a few examples of what I mean from past MBE questions:

MBE SAMPLE QUESTION #3

Penstock owned a large tract of land on the shore of a lake. Drury lived on a stream that ran along one boundary of Penstock's land and into the lake. At some time in the past, a channel had been cut across Penstock's land from the stream to the lake at a point some distance from the mouth of the stream. From where Drury lived, the channel served as a convenient shortcut to the lake. Erroneously believing that the channel was a public waterway, Drury made frequent trips through the channel in his motorboat. His use of the channel caused no harm to the land through which it passed.

If Penstock asserts a claim for damages against Drury based on trespass, which of the following would be a correct disposition of the case?

A. Judgment for Penstock for nominal damages, because Drury intentionally used the channel.

B. Judgment for Drury, if he did not use the channel after learning of Penstock's ownership claim.

C. Judgment for Drury, because he caused no harm to Penstock's land.

D. Judgment for Drury, because when he used the channel he believed it was a public waterway.

MBE SAMPLE QUESTION #4

Pawn sued Dalton for injuries received when she fell down a stairway in Dalton's apartment building. Pawn, a guest in the building, alleged that she caught the heel of her shoe in a tear in the stair carpet. Pawn calls Witt, a tenant, to testify that Young, another tenant, had said to him a week before Pawn's fall: "When I paid my rent this morning, I told the manager he had better fix that torn carpet."

Young's statement, reported by Witt, is

A. admissible, to prove that the carpet was defective.

B. admissible, to prove that Dalton had notice of the defect.

C. admissible, to prove both that the carpet was defective and that Dalton had notice of the defect.

D. inadmissible, because it is hearsay not within any exception.

The two questions above are examples of what I call a "three-to-one split." In both cases, the "stand alone" conclusion is correct. (In Question 3, A is the correct answer; and D is the correct answer in Question 4.) I am, of course, in no way telling you to automatically choose the stand alone answer choice on the MBE. All I am saying is that you should in no way be predisposed to assume that the correct answer will come from the side with the three similar outcomes.

(5) A More Precise Answer Is Usually Better than a Less Precise Answer

A more "precise" answer is a "better" (and therefore "more correct") answer. A more precise answer either (a) incorporates more facts, (b) covers more issues raised from the question, or (c) gives more reasoning. Here are a few very basic examples:

Example 6-1 from Criminal Law:

A) The defendant is not guilty of any crime.
B) The defendant is guilty of a crime because he killed the victim.
C) The defendant is guilty of manslaughter.
D) The defendant is guilty of manslaughter because he killed the victim in the heat of passion.

Example 6-2 from Evidence:

A) The evidence is inadmissible.
B) The evidence is admissible.
C) The evidence is admissible even though it is hearsay.
D) The evidence is admissible under the excited utterance exception to the hearsay rule.

In both examples the last answer is more precise, and thus, technically "more correct" than the other three. (Of course, D may or may not be more correct vis-à-vis Answer A, which has a different result.) Accordingly, D is a better choice than B or C. Below is an example of a more "precise answer" being a "better" answer choice (also from an actual MBE released question):

MBE SAMPLE QUESTION #5

Loomis, the owner and operator of a small business, encourages "wellness" on the part of his employees and supports various physical-fitness programs to that end. Learning that one of his employees, Graceful, was a dedicated jogger, Loomis promised to pay her a special award of $100 if she could and would run one mile in less than six minutes on the following Saturday. Graceful thanked him, and did in fact run a mile in less than six minutes on the day specified. Shortly thereafter, however, Loomis discovered that for more than a year Graceful had been running at least one mile in less than six minutes every day as a part of her personal fitness program. He refused to pay the $100.

In an action by Graceful against Loomis for breach of contract, which of the following best summarizes the probable decision of the court?

A. Loomis wins, because it is a compelling inference that Loomis' promise did not induce Graceful to run the specified mile.

B. Loomis wins, because Graceful's running of the specified mile was beneficial, not detrimental, to her in any event.

C. Graceful wins, because running a mile in less than six minutes is a significantly demanding enterprise.

D. Graceful wins, because she ran the specified mile as requested, and her motives for doing so are irrelevant.

The correct answer is Answer D. Notice how Answer D is more precise—it gives two reasons for why Graceful wins. The other answers only give one reason as to why the court should rule a certain way.

In no way should you base your initial strategy on selecting the more precise answer, but if you come to a sticking point in your analysis, you are more likely to be correct by picking the more precise answer.

(6) Be Very Leery of Absolutes

As you probably know after three years of law school, there are very few absolutes in the law. Thus, there are few absolutes on the MBE. As such, be wary of answers that state absolutes with words such as "always" or "never."

(7) Focus on Conjunctions

There are four types of conjunctions that you might encounter on the MBE. It's important to know exactly what each one means when breaking down each answer choice. The four types of conjunctions important in this context are: because, if, only if, and unless. Let me break down what each means as it pertains to the MBE answer choices:

BECAUSE

The conjunction "because" is the most common type of connector on the MBE. Here's an example of an answer choice with "because" as its conjunction:

John will likely prevail because he was unaware of the agreement.

As you can see, the word "because" connects the conclusion with a specific reason for that conclusion. Accordingly, for an answer choice to be the correct answer, both the conclusion ("John will prevail") must be correct, and the reason supporting the conclusion ("because he was unaware of the agreement") must be correct.

IF

There's one big thing to remember about the "if" conjunction: the fact that is contained in the "if" answer choice does *not* have to appear in the actual fact pattern. The "if" connector hypothesizes about a new fact not contained in the original fact pattern. Here's an example of an answer choice containing "if":

> John will prevail if he was unaware of the agreement.

For an answer choice to be correct when it contains the conjunction "if" requires that the focus of inquiry be narrowed to whether or not the entire statement is true, with the assumption that the proposition which follows the "if" is true. BUT there is no requirement that facts in the fact pattern support the proposition following the "if" connector.

ONLY IF

The "only if" conjunction is basically the same as the "if" conjunction, but when "only if" is used, the answer choice cannot be correct except when the condition following the word "if" is true. Here's an example:

> John will prevail only if he was unaware of the agreement.

Thus, in the above example, the "only if" connector denotes that the only possible way John can prevail is by showing he was unaware of the agreement. If John can prevail in some other manner in addition to being unaware of the agreement, the above answer choice would be incorrect.

UNLESS

The conjunction "unless" performs the same logical function as the conjunction "only if" except that it precedes a negative exclusive condition instead of a positive one.

> John will not prevail unless he was unaware of the agreement.

The above example is the same as the example containing the "only if" connector, but it is stated in the negative (by adding the "not" in front of "prevail"). Regardless, the meaning is the same:

John can only prevail if he was unaware of the agreement—and there can be no other means by which he could prevail.

(8) When All Else Fails—Choose the Longest Answer

I only recommend this as a last resort, but if you are at a complete loss as to the correct answer, consider choosing the longer answer. All other things being equal, a longer answer probably contains more reasoning—thereby likely making it more "correct." (Note that this tip is closely related to Tip #5: an answer that is more precise or contains more reasoning is usually longer than other answers.) And if you couldn't eliminate it by other means, and it's a choice between two (or even three) answers, pick the longer one. Again—when I say "longer" I mean "more reasoning." Here are a few examples, both of which are actual released questions:

MBE SAMPLE QUESTION #6

The United States Department of Energy regularly transports nuclear materials through Centerville on the way to a nuclear weapons processing plant it operates in a nearby state. The city of Centerville recently adopted an ordinance prohibiting the transportation of any nuclear materials in or through the city. The ordinance declares that its purpose is to protect the health and safety of the residents of that city.

May the Department of Energy continue to transport these nuclear materials through the city of Centerville?

A. No, because the ordinance is rationally related to the public health and safety of Centerville residents.

B. No, because the Tenth Amendment reserves to the states certain unenumerated sovereign powers.

C. Yes, because the Department of Energy is a federal agency engaged in a lawful federal function and, therefore, its activities may not be regulated by a local government without the consent of Congress.

D. Yes, because the ordinance enacted by Centerville is invalid because it denies persons transporting such materials the equal protection of the laws.

In the above example, C is the correct answer. It happens to be the "longest" answer, but it (more importantly) has more reasoning than the other choices (which makes it "longer").

If we enumerate the "reasons" behind each answer, we see that only Answer C actually contains two reasons after the causal connector "because": (1) the Department of Energy is a federal agency engaged in a lawful federal function, and (2) its activities may not be regulated by a local government without the consent of Congress. The other answer choices only offer one reason for their reasoning.

Here is another example from a released question:

MBE SAMPLE QUESTION #7

Which of the following fact patterns most clearly suggests an implied-in-fact contract?
A. A county tax assessor mistakenly bills Algernon for taxes on Bathsheba's property, which Algernon, in good faith, pays.
B. Meddick, a physician, treated Ryder without Ryder's knowledge or consent, while Ryder was unconscious as the result of a fall from his horse.
C. Asphalt, thinking that he was paving Customer's driveway, for which Asphalt had an express contract, mistakenly paved Nabor's driveway while Nabor looked on without saying anything or raising any objection.
D. At her mother's request, Iris, an accountant, filled out and filed her mother's "E-Z" income-tax form (a simple, short form).

In the above example, C is the correct answer. Again, it is the "longest" answer—and the one containing the most relevant information to the issue of an implied-in-fact contract. I would like to reiterate that this "tip" should only be used when you are stuck and have exhausted all other avenues of deciding the answer. Choosing the "longest" answer should only be used as a last resort.

No matter how prepared you are, no matter how many practice questions you do, no matter how well you know the law, you will have to guess during the MBE. The key is to make intelligent, educated guesses. And you do that by going through all of the processes that we have talked about and eliminating as many answer choices as you can.

(9) Ask the Universe

As I've stated previously, the true goal of Zen—enlightenment— is to know the true nature of yourself and the true nature of the oneness of all things. If you have practiced Zen leading up to the bar, you may find that your intuition has improved dramatically. After all, many people (and most religions) believe that we are "born of" God/the universe/source energy (or whatever semantic label you want to put on it), and that this source from which we come is all-knowing. Accordingly, the more we practice knowing the true nature of ourselves, the more we are connected to the all-knowing divinity/spirit/energy. Intuition exists—we just need to practice trying to tap into it.

Thus, if you have studied a particular MBE question, exhausted all of the tips I have outlined above, and you still don't have a clue as to the correct answer, then clear your mind completely and ask the universe what the correct answer is. If an answer pops into your mind (and trust me, if you can truly blank your mind for a moment, an answer *will* come), go with that answer and move on. Hey, the universe always knows—you just have to be willing to listen.

(10) After Each Question, Let It Go

As noted on the section on essay writing, it is absolutely critical to "let go" of an answer after you have moved on to the next one. Again, lingering thoughts about a particular question will only take your focus away from the next question. And FOCUS and CON-CENTRATION throughout the exam are keys to getting a passing score.

What the NCBE Says

I have given you my top ten tips, but now I'd like to give you NCBE's "Top Three." According to the NCBE, studies have shown that the top three reasons for incorrect answers on MBE multiple choice questions are:

(1)   Errors in knowing or understanding legal principles (you have to know the law).

(2)   Errors in assuming facts or reading non-existing facts into the fact pattern.

(3)   Not responding to the specific call of the question.

7. Handling Negativity and Bumps Along the Path

When life becomes difficult,
allow yourself to feel the pain in the moment. Go with it for
as long as it lasts, and then **allow it to dissolve away***. Pain is*
merely a state of mind, rather than a situation.
Every situation is neutral.

Having tutored and lectured for the bar exam for the past several years, I am well aware that most students experience periods of negativity and/or anxiety during the rigorous process of studying for the bar exam. It's inevitable, so do your best to accept the negative moments and allow them to dissolve away. And this is the key: **allow them** to dissolve away — do not hold onto that which does not serve you.

Below I have pinpointed some of the reasons why negative moments might creep in, and I offer advice (couched in Zen philosophy) as to how to maintain your balance and move forward on your path to enlightenment.

Negative Feeling: Fear of Failure

Fear debilitates.
When we're scared, we stand like a deer caught in the
headlights: not able to move away from the very thing that
frightens us. To escape fear, all we have to do is keep moving.

Fear of failing the bar exam is a common thought that is bound to creep into your vibration at some point. Acknowledge the fear, accept it as natural, and move on. Don't become paralyzed by the fear and feed its appetite; keep moving along your path. If the fear of failure becomes particularly intense, I suggest moving along with a subject you know well. Return to studying one of your best known subjects and get a little of your confidence back. Remember — all you have to do is keep moving along the path.

Negative Feeling: I Cannot Learn All of This Information in Time

If you understand, things are just as they are ...
if you do not understand, things are just as they are.

The truth is, you will not be able to understand every single concept tested on the bar exam. You will not be able to learn every single rule, exception to every rule, extension of every rule. It is a virtually impossible task given the small amount of time you have to study. Fortunately, you don't have to learn every single rule or understand every single legal concept; you just have to know enough to pass. Whether you understand the rule of perpetuities or not, things are still just as they are. Accept that you cannot possibly learn everything; learn what you can and keep moving forward.

☯ ☯ ☯

Negative Feeling: I'm Missing Issues or Not Getting Enough MBEs Correct

Understand the yin and the yang.
Within the white is a dot of black,
and within the black
is a dot of white.
Nothing is ever absolutely perfect;
therefore, be happy
with the imperfection
of your own being.

You are not perfect — no one is. Accept this imperfection and know that you are not going to spot every single issue, and you are not going to get every single MBE question correct. What you are looking for is improvement. But do realize that there will likely be days when you are a little "off" and not doing as well (on either essays or MBE questions or both) as you had previously. Don't dwell on this — it's only a step back if you perceive it to be a step back. We all have off days. Accept the imperfection of an off day, and you will help maintain the balance of mind, body, and spirit that you will need along the path to passing.

Above all, resist any temptation to "beat yourself up" over how you are doing. Don't ever allow yourself to say that you aren't smart enough, or that you can't pass the exam. Don't ever judge yourself based on how you do on any given MBE study session or series of practice essays.

Live life with an open heart.
Erase judgment from your thoughts,
live with compassion, and practice
understanding. Keep in mind
that everyone is doing the best
they possibly can and realize
that if they knew better,
they'd do better — therefore,
be gentle. ***Now, practice this***
same gentleness with yourself.
Know that you're doing the best
you can in every situation
and ***honor yourself with compassion.***
This simple thought will help you be less
critical and more appreciative
of all that is.

Negative Feeling: I Just Don't Understand Property [Or Other Subject(s)]

Be thankful for anyone
in your life who's a problem.
They're your teachers, for they show
you where you truly stand. A great saint once
said to a disciple who came to him complaining
about someone else: "He is your greatest blessing.
In fact, if he were not here, it would behoove
us to go out and find one like him."

Be thankful for the subjects that you "don't get" or "can't stand." Everyone has at least one of these subjects—and oftentimes more than one. These are the subjects that will push you, challenge you, and give you the opportunity to evolve and know your true self. Remember: the harder you push against something, the harder it will push back.

Don't expect to practice hard and not experience the weird. Hard practice that evades the unknown makes for a weak commitment. So an ancient once said, "Help hard practice by befriending every demon."

As a matter of practical advice, if you have a particularly difficult subject, start with the basics. Figure out what are the most commonly tested issues from past exams. Use that as your starting point. Next, try a study aid. Hornbooks are great for immersing yourself in a subject and getting a feel for how concepts are interrelated. Of course, you can also ask your peers or old law school professors for recommendations on specific sources. Sometimes, talking through it with someone who has a good grasp on the subject can make things click, too.

Two other pieces of advice: first, don't spend an inordinate amount of time on a subject you "don't get." Don't neglect the subjects you know well. The bar exam is all about accumulating points and you don't want to spend considerably more time trying to "get" one subject to the detriment of other subjects. As Nietzsche so famously said, "If you look too deeply into the abyss, the abyss will look into you." Instead, try the opposite....

Become
as a little child,
seeing all things for the first time.

Second, stop telling yourself that you "don't get" Property (or other subject) because this simply reinforces your belief (and will make it more difficult to overcome). Instead, try to approach the subject as if you are experiencing it for the first time. Oftentimes, the people I tutor tell me they have a hang up about a subject because of a poor grade they received in law school or because a professor whom they despised taught that particular subject. If this is the case, just remember—both the grade and the professor happened in the past. Try to view the subject as if a little child—see it for the first time.

If the clean slate approach doesn't work for you, and you still find yourself "lost" or feeling negativity about a particular subject, change your thoughts about it. Instead of saying you "don't get Property," say "I'm glad Property is challenging because I'll feel that much better when I do get it." Or say, "Property is challenging me right now, *but I will get it.*" Remember Daniel Levin's poignant question I mentioned earlier: why do we think that it's only the things we do that matter and not the things we think?

⚘ ⚘ ⚘

Negative Feeling: Other People are Studying Way More Than I Am

If you see the Buddha on the road, kill him.

The quote above is a famous Buddhist quote that has been interpreted in many ways over the years. To me, the quote has always meant that one should not have a preconceived notion of what it means to be an enlightened being. "Enlightenment" is different for everyone—and so is the path. You are your own Buddha, and everyone must take their own path to find his or her nirvana. Trying to emulate someone else will never bring you your own enlightenment.

Accordingly, as it pertains to the bar exam: don't try to emulate the study habits of someone you think is "on the right path" to passing the exam. Be your own Buddha. Someone else's study habits may not be right for you. Don't concern yourself if Joey Joe-Joe is studying twenty hours a day and taking five different review courses.

It truly is about quality over quantity. What does it mean to have "quality" study sessions? A "quality" study session is one where you are completely present, completely mindful of what you are doing. We are all different learners and have different avenues for studying most effectively. Follow your own path, and do not be influenced by what others are doing. You are your own Buddha!

The
river flows,
the mountain
remains motionless.
The river can't remain still, nor can the mountain flow.
Is one right or wrong? Our **dharma** *(duty) is to do*
what's ours to do, not to be like others.

☯ ☯ ☯

Negative Feeling: Overall Anxiety (Or Even Feeling Sick to Your Stomach)

Breathe.
Your breath is the greatest tool you have
to help you know exactly where you
are. The quicker your breath, the more
agitated you are; the deeper your breath,
the more relaxed you are. Therefore, to
relax in any moment, take six long, deep
breaths in and out.

As I alluded to earlier, anxiety is a normal part of the bar exam journey (and can result from any of the negative thoughts noted above). Virtually everyone experiences anxiety at some point—while others experience it on a daily basis. The key is to be aware that you are having anxiety, then having the awareness of how to handle it.

First—release all thoughts from your mind. Close your eyes and focus on your breath. Be present with your breath. If a thought comes, accept it, then let it go, and return to focusing on your breath. After a few long deep inhales, you will feel a little better. Keep breathing until your anxiety has lessened; then smile. Keep breathing and (if you have to) force yourself to smile. The physical act of smiling—even if you force yourself to smile—has been shown to have the same positive physiological affects that occur during a spontaneous smile.[10]

If you would like to take this a step farther, take a minute or two (or longer if you can) to express gratitude for all that you have in your life (health, family, friends, pets, shelter, food, a vehicle, a law degree, etc.). Smile—I'm sure you have a lot to be thankful for. The more you do this exercise, the easier it will be to let go of anxiety the next time it arises. Use your breath to ground you in the present moment whenever you can. It will increase your mindfulness and give you greater perspective in any situation.

Of course, I invite you to make meditation a daily part of your path. Yes, your time will be at a premium, but the most important time to relax is when you feel as if you have no time to relax. A Zen-mind has no distractions and stress/anxiety can be an enormous distraction to your focus. Numerous studies have shown that meditation not only significantly reduces stress/anxiety, but it can also have a profoundly positive physiological effect on the body, including helping to reverse heart disease, reduce pain, and enhance the body's immune system.[11]

---

10. *See generally*, Ekman and Davidson, *Voluntary Smiling Changes Regional Brain Activity*, 4 PSYCHOL. SCI. 5 (Sept. 1993).

11. S. Praissman, *Mindfulness-based Stress Reduction: A Literature Review and Clinician's Guide*, 20 J. Am. Acad. Nurse Pract., 212, 212–16 (2008); *see*

If you choose to meditate, it doesn't have to be for very long. Even a few minutes a day can yield positive results for your mind, body, and soul (and of course stress reduction). There are many different types of meditation, but the goal is always the same — reduce stress (and tune into your true self) by checking out of the anxiety-driven, clutter-filled, non-present thoughts of the mind. Some meditations focus on breathing, while others focus on repeating a word or phrase over and over ("I will pass the bar exam"). How do you know if you are doing it correctly? If you feel better when you are done.

Breathe. Breathe again.
Breathe in peace, breathe out anxiety. Breathe. Breathe again.
Breathe in love,
breathe out hatred. Breathe. Breathe again. Breathe in
thoughts of success,
and breathe out thoughts of failure.

---

also, Shauna L. Shapiro, et al., *Cultivating Mindfulness: Effects on Well-being,* 64 J. CLINICAL PSYCHOL. 840, 840–62 (2008); *see generally,* Cary Barbor, *The Science of Meditation,* PSYCHOL. TODAY, May/June 2001.

8. Knowing Your Universe

The Buddha mind contains the universe.

Before the Exam — Know Your Location

If you have to travel to the exam, be sure to get your hotel (or other accommodations) *early*. Be sure to do a "dry run" from your hotel (or residence) to the exam location to see how long it takes to get there. Be sure to do this at the same time you will be traveling to get a feel for traffic at that particular time.

If at all possible, check out the room of the exam location beforehand. It will help you to visualize yourself doing well prior to exam day. It will also give you a "feel" for the place — both energetically and temperature wise. Although they will tell you on the day of the exam, it would also be helpful to know exactly where the bathrooms are located.

Before the Exam — Know the Rules of Protocol

If you don't know the rules, it could cost you. Every state has specific rules, so be sure to follow them — both before and during the exam. Every year there are examinees who (apparently inadvertently) take part of their exam past a restricted area and are immediately disqualified from taking the exam.

Another rule to keep in mind — do not bring your cell phone! You should get a complete list of all of the rules after you have sent in your application and fee to sit for the bar exam. Read the rules a few times before the exam, know the rules, and abide by them.

The Day of the Exam

It's game time, so put on your game face. Hopefully, you took my advice and cut down on the caffeine during the lead-up to the exam. It's an awful idea to load up on caffeine the morning of the exam. For one, you will experience the caffeine "crash" right around the middle of the first exam session. Also, you don't want to waste time taking multiple bathroom breaks during the exam.

Eat well, but not too much. The earlier you eat, the better. You want to give your food time to digest before sitting down for three hours of thinking and writing (mindfully being present).

Wear comfortable clothes. You don't want to be distracted because you are cold (or hot). That is why long pants (sweats, khakis, comfortable jeans) and layers on top work well. If you take the exam during July, many places will blast the air conditioning and it might be colder than you think in the examination room. Do what you can to ensure you aren't distracted by things such as temperature.

Be present when you begin your first essay. (Day one of the exam is normally the essay day for most states.) Generally speaking, answer the questions in the order you get them. You don't want to waste time sifting through the questions to answer the subject you know "best."

There is, however, one exception to this rule: if there is a subject that gives you an absolute mental block, you might want to consider moving that subject to the end when it comes up. It's important to start off with as positive of a first step as you can, so if you are absolutely hung up on Constitutional Law (or other subject), consider saving it until the end. Moreover, if you do run out of time, it's better to run out of time on a subject that you don't know very well.

You should **not**, however, sift through each essay and try to rank the questions in a particular order; nor should you try to search out a particular subject in order to answer it first (or last). Doing so will cost you valuable time, and you will need all the time you can get. Answer the questions in order, and if/when you come across the subject you aren't comfortable with, feel free to put that essay off until the end.

On the first break, remember to stay present. Don't worry about past essays; let them go. Bring your outlines with you so that you can go over the remaining subjects during the two-hour lunch break. Speaking of lunch, be sure to again eat well—eat something healthy, not too filling. Avoid foods that make you sleepy (turkey, milk, etc.). Moreover, avoid talking about the first session with your friends. Doing so will only feed potential anxiety.

After Day 1, take some time to decompress. You will be doing yourself a disservice if you immediately start studying for the next day's MBE exam. Try to relax, clear your mind, have a good (healthy) dinner. And, above all else, don't look back. In fact, make it a point to avoid anyone who wants to talk to you about specific questions or "issues" from the essay portion of the exam. Get a good night's sleep and stay positive. Regardless of how you think you did during the first day, let it go. Stay present. I know it may be a daunting task, but do your best to be optimistic and appreciate that you "get to" participate in day two of the bar exam the next morning.

Upon waking for the next day of the exam, it's even more important to eat well and not over-caffeinate. If day two is your state's MBE day, I suggest doing five to ten MBE questions to get your mind prepared for the task ahead. BUT DO NOT, under any circumstance, check the answers! You don't want to undermine your confidence; the goal is to just re-orient your brain on the MBE process.

During the exam, be present with each question and let your preparation guide you along the path. Follow the same "meditation" for answering each question in the same manner you have practiced: read the call of the question, read the facts, spot issues, eliminate answer choices, etc. Stay positive and have gratitude for the privilege of experiencing the 200-question journey. ☺

The attainment of completeness calls for the use of the whole. Nothing less will do; hence there can be no easier conditions, no substitution, no compromise.
— Zen Master D.T. Suzuki

There are no shortcuts to enlightenment. Your complete focus — mind, body, and soul — need to work in unison. This is the way of Zen. So study hard, practice correctly, eat well, exercise, sleep well, be present, be simple, be positive, be confident, be kind to yourself . . . and pass the bar exam. Good luck — and happy passing.

9. After the Exam

Learning Zen is a phenomenon of gold and dung.
Before you understand it, it's like gold;
after you understand it, it's like dung.
— *Zen Master*

I told you Zen was akin to studying for the bar exam! Enjoy your dung—you've earned it. To ensure you enjoy yourself, fight the urge to discuss the exam or go back over some of the issues. This will only cause you increased anxiety—and you will not be living in the present. Put positive thoughts of passing the exam into the universe and enjoy your career as a lawyer. Visualize the good you can do (for yourself, your family, the world) with your licensure. Accordingly....

When you get to the top of the mountain, keep climbing.

☯   ☯   ☯

Appendix A
A Note to Repeat Takers

Help hard practice by befriending every demon.

It is my sincere hope that you do not have to read this section. If you did not pass the exam, you can pass the next time—or even the time after that. (I tutored one person who had failed four times before he came to me, and then passed the fifth time with points to spare.) Taking the exam again can be extremely challenging, and the bar exam may now truly have become a "demon." Do your best to accept the situation, have gratitude that you have another opportunity, and befriend the demon.

There are two critical things to do in order to pass as a repeat taker. First, let go of the stigma or embarrassment you might feel because you didn't pass the exam. You are not alone—thousands of people across the country are unsuccessful the first, second, or even third time they take the exam. In many states, as many as 45–50% or more of examinees do not pass.

Having to retake the bar exam should *in no way* be equated with your level of intelligence. Most people fail the exam because they don't know how to take the time-pressured test. If you made it into law school and graduated, you are smart enough to pass the exam. Let go of any hit to your confidence or ego, and learn how to study correctly, and how to actually take the exam. Learn to be present and increase your focus and concentration. I hope this book has helped in these endeavors.

A plant
needs sunshine
and rain
in order to grow,
just as all beings need love and
suffering to grow. Therefore,
when suffering comes, drink
it in like water and allow it to
make you more beautiful.

I realize it's incredibly difficult to think that re-taking the bar exam will have positive benefits, but it will. You will learn the law better, you will learn more about the resolve and fortitude that you have deep within, you will become stronger (and, yes, as the above quote notes, you can even become more beautiful through the process). Resolve that you will pass, and approach the exam as if it will reap positive benefits.

If you want to pass this time, it's even more important to apply one of our main Zen principles — know yourself. Whatever you do differently, it is absolutely critical that you pinpoint your weaknesses on your old exam. Find out as much as you can about what went wrong. Ask yourself: How did your MBE score compare with your essay score? Is there a high correlation between the two, or were you completely deficient in one area and not the other? How much did exam day anxiety factor into your performance?

Regardless of your essay scores (even if they were high), you want to improve in every area you can. To that end, as quickly as possible, contact your state's Bar Examiners and order copies of your old essays. From there, it should be relatively obvious where you went wrong — was it issue spotting, knowing the law, or applying the law? Most of the time, it's some combination thereof, but you should be able to isolate the biggest problem. (If not, perhaps consider hiring a tutor to help figure it out.)

Ask yourself this question: did I truly know the law? If the answer is yes, then perhaps writing the analysis is the area you need to improve the most. Whenever possible, try to look for "model" answers. Some states release model answers, and you can often find "model" answers from bar review courses.

Remember, many people fail the bar exam and pass the second (or third, or fourth) time around. And you can, too. If you want it badly enough, and if you believe it strongly enough, you will pass this time around.

The storms of life come and go...
Earthquakes, tornadoes, and hurricanes cause destruction, and
then over time, the earth heals itself. Be like the earth: Walk
through the tragedies of life, and then **as soon as
possible, rebuild yourself.**

Appendix B
The Energy Notebook

When the window was dirty, the man couldn't see through it; when the window was clean, he couldn't see the window. The beauty of the window was that he couldn't see it. The beauty of the Zen mind is that it causes no interference.

The Energy Notebook

Aside from the techniques I have already referred to, I often recommend an "energy notebook" for learning all of the rules of law. Get a notebook—make it a special notebook. Put pictures of your family, pets, favorite people or things on the front and give the notebook positive energy. (If you have kids or a significant other, a great thing to do is have them write in the notebook on the inside cover.) Yes—I'm serious about this. The notebook has to be one of reverence and positive energy (or you will more easily grow to resent it, which will only undermine the learning).

Most people go through their outlines when they try to learn the law. They will go through a particular subject, and try to repeat the rule of law for the particular sub-topics. Often, especially early on, you won't get all of the rules correct. That's when the energy notebook comes into play. Every time you "miss" a rule of law, write it down verbatim in your notebook—and *be mindfully present* as you do this.

This process forces your mind to work on different levels, thereby increasing your likelihood of remembering the full rule the next time around—especially if you're truly mindful when you undertake your task. Specifically, it forces you into active learning—recalling the rule and physically writing it down. The physical act of writing out the rule calls upon the brain to engage on a second level (rather than just reading the rule you missed), which adds strength to your brain's neurotransmitters (and thus makes it more likely to remember the rule in the future).

Always write down the date and subject in your notebook when you start your "rule learning" session. This will give you a good idea of where you stand as you get closer to exam day because you can immediately tell how much of the law you still don't know (and how much you do know) at various intervals of studying. In an ideal world, the number of rules you write in your notebook will be far fewer as you get closer to the exam date.

Moreover, the energy notebook will be a good study aid in the final week of the exam. Rather than trying to review your (potentially) lengthy outlines a day or days before the exam, you can just review the rules in the recent entries of your notebook. Do note that, at first, it may be a daunting task to memorialize the rules you "miss" by writing them all down, but if you stick with it, you should find that you are learning all the rules faster than you were when just reading over your outlines. Also, I suggest waiting until you are at least relatively familiar with the particular subject you are studying before you start to write entries in your notebook.

Work is love made visible. And if you cannot work with love but only with distaste, it is better that you should leave your work and sit at the gate of the temple and take alms of those who work with joy.

— Kahlil Gibran

Appendix C
Additional Exercises for Essay Writing

We do not learn by experience, but by our capacity for experience.
— the Buddha

Below are additional short exercises you can use to practice writing out essay issues. I have provided a short fact pattern and the relevant rules for issues raised from the facts. I invite you to increase your capacity for experience: take a few minutes, focus on being present, and write out short answers to the following exercises. I have also provided model answers for each essay.

Think of each "issue" as a mini-essay. And, remember: there are many ways to write out an answer and receive maximum credit; the model answers I provide are merely one (simple) way to maximize your score.

Exercise C-1 (Criminal Procedure)

Facts:

Officer Arnold is in his patrol car running radar when he clocks Bert's car speeding past him at 15 miles over the speed limit. Officer Arnold turns on his siren and lights and chases Bert's speeding car. Bert pulls his vehicle over after seeing the squad car. Officer Arnold approaches Bert's car and issues Bert a citation for speeding. Then without Bert's consent, Officer Arnold searches the interior of Bert's car. The search turns up a substantial quantity of cocaine hidden under the car's front seat.

Officer Arnold places Bert under arrest for cocaine possession, handcuffs Bert, and takes Bert to the police station. Upon reaching the police station, Arnold, suspecting Bert of being involved in a large illegal drug operation, rigorously questions Bert about such involvement without informing Bert of his *Miranda* rights and disregarding Bert's requests for a lawyer.

Bert eventually made incriminating statements about his involvement in the drug operation. Will Bert's statements be admissible at trial?

Relevant rule:

Miranda rights are required whenever a person is in custodial interrogation. One is considered to be in custody if placed under arrest or reasonably believes he is not free to leave. Interrogation exists when police words or conduct are likely to elicit an incriminating response.

Model Answers to Exercise C-1

Model Answer #1:

Miranda Violation

Miranda rights are required whenever a person is in custodial interrogation. One is considered to be in custody if placed under arrest or reasonably believes he is not free to leave. Interrogation exists when police words or conduct are likely to elicit an incriminating response.

In the facts at bar, the Officer pulled Bert over for speeding and searched his car. After this, he handcuffed Bert and took Bert to the police station. At the police station, the Officer rigorously questioned Bert about his involvement in an illegal drug ring in the area. Accordingly, Bert was most likely in custodial interrogation and should have been read his *Miranda* rights. Because he was not read his *Miranda* rights, the incriminating statements will not be admissible at Bert's trial.

Model Answer #2:

Miranda Violation

Miranda rights are required whenever a person is in custodial interrogation. One is considered to be in custody if placed under arrest or reasonably believes he is not free to leave. Interrogation exists when police words or conduct are likely to elicit an incriminating response.

Here, Bert was in custody (not reasonably free to leave) because the Officer put him in handcuffs and took him to the station for questioning. Also, the Officer interrogated Bert because he "rigorously questioned" him about his "involvement in an illegal drug ring" in the area. Thus, custodial interrogation took place and Bert should have been read his *Miranda* rights. The evidence will not be admissible at Bert's trial.

Discussion of Model Answers to Exercise C-1

Hopefully, your answer more closely resembles Model Answer #2. Again, Model Answer #1 is an example of reciting facts and not showing all of the writer's work. Model Answer #2 matches up (integrates) facts with parts of the rule and is clearly a better analysis. Also, note the parenthetical short cut defining "custody" in #2.

If you lose the spirit of repetition,
your practice will become quite difficult.
    — Zen Master Shunryu Suzuki

☯   ☯   ☯

Exercise C-2 (Criminal Procedure)

Facts:

Joe was out for his morning walk when he noticed a police officer walking toward him. Joe looked away, hoping to avoid eye contact because he was carrying an ounce of marijuana in his pocket. The officer stepped in front of Joe, grabbed Joe's arm and said, "Hey, I need to ask you a few questions." Joe, continuing to look away, replied, "Sorry, bro—I'm in a real hurry" and tried to step around the officer. The officer grabbed onto Joe's arm and said, "This won't take long and it's important."

Joe stopped and looked up at the officer. The officer looked Joe up and down and then asked, "Where's the closest doughnut shop around here?" Joe threw his hands into the air and blurted out, "I'm just selling the weed to pay off my law school loans!"

Joe was arrested and charged with intent to distribute a controlled substance. Joe's attorney has moved to suppress Joe's statement. How should the court rule?

Relevant rule:

Miranda rights are required whenever a person is in custodial interrogation. One is considered to be in custody if placed under arrest or reasonably believes he is not free to leave. Interrogation exists when police words or conduct are likely to elicit an incriminating response. A spontaneous statement made by the defendant does not constitute interrogation.

Model Answers to Exercise C-2

Model Answer #1:

Miranda Violation

Miranda rights are required whenever a person is in custodial interrogation. One is considered to be in custody if placed under arrest or reasonably believes he is not free to leave. Interrogation exists when police words or conduct are likely to elicit an incriminating response. A spontaneous statement made by the defendant does not constitute interrogation.

Here Joe may or may not have been in custody at the time—but he likely was in custody because he likely did not feel free to leave in such a situation. However, the fact of custody doesn't matter because there was likely not an interrogation based on the facts that were given in the fact pattern. A spontaneous statement does not constitute interrogation. If there is not interrogation then there is no custodial interrogation and thus there is no requirement for giving *Miranda* rights. Accordingly, the statement was not made in violation of Joe's *Miranda* rights.

Model Answer #2:

Miranda Violation

Miranda rights are required whenever a person is in custodial interrogation. One is considered to be in custody if placed under arrest or reasonably believes he is not free to leave. Interrogation exists when police words or conduct are likely to elicit an incriminating response. A spontaneous statement made by the defendant does not constitute interrogation.

Here, Joe was likely in custody (not free to leave) because the officer stepped in front of Joe and grabbed onto his arm when Joe tried to leave. However, the officer likely did not interrogate Joe because his question, "Where's the closest doughnut shop" is not one likely to elicit an incriminating response. Moreover, Joe's statement about selling weed was a spontaneous statement because he "blurted" it out (and spontaneous statements are not interrogation). Thus, the court should not suppress Joe's statement.

If you have chosen not to write out an answer (or even if you have), I invite you to fully answer this question: Which answer is better — *and why?*

Discussion of Model Answers to Exercise C-2

Hopefully, you are now able to recognize that Model Answer #2 is far better. Answer #1 is an example of a "law-based" answer, discussed more fully in Chapter 2. It is full of "legal conclusion" sentences and includes virtually no facts within the analysis. Remember — there can be no analysis without applying facts to rules.

Answer #1 is actually the type of answer I have often seen — a little hurried, a little rambling, but one that is attempting to "show all of the work" by trying to "spell things out" from point A to point B. But upon closer analysis, it is clear as to why Answer #2 is much better.

Another minor point — the conclusion in Answer #1 does not *specifically* answer the call of the question as to whether the statement should be suppressed. Again, it seems clear the writer knows the answer, but we never want to make the grader guess. If the question asks whether the statement should be suppressed, then your conclusion should specifically address this point.

One final note on the "rule" I outlined for the Model Answers in C-2. Unlike the Model Answers in Exercise C-1 (Officer Arnold and Bert), I included the additional part of the rule regarding the "spontaneous statement" here. I didn't include this part of the rule (more appropriately called a "rule explanation") in the previous exercise because it wasn't relevant. It is, however, relevant to this exercise, so I have included it.

☯   ☯   ☯

Exercise C-3 (Torts)

Facts:

ACME Corp. has a company Board meeting once a month. There are six board members, as follows: Al, Betty, Carol, Dave, Ellen, and Fred. On June 23, all board members were present at the meeting start time of 9:00 a.m. except Ellen. Finally, at 9:05, Dave stood up and said, "I'm sure Ellen's late because she's a drug addict. I don't think she's fit to be a member of this board."

Five minutes later, Ellen walked in, and was summarily shunned by other members of the board. When she attempted to give input on business matters, her opinion was quickly dismissed, which Ellen thought odd because she had always been a highly respected board member.

A week later, Ellen found out about Dave's comment to the board, which he had only made to get back at Ellen because she had rebuffed his advances at a company happy hour on June 20. Ellen wants to sue Dave. Under what theories of recovery could she sue Dave, and what is her likelihood of winning?

Relevant rule:

The relevant rule for defamation is as follows: defamatory language of or concerning the Plaintiff, publication to a third person, and damage to the Plaintiff's reputation.

Model Answer to Exercise C-3

<u>Defamation</u>
Defamation is actionable when there is defamatory language that is of or concerning the Plaintiff, publication to a third party, and damage to the Plaintiff's reputation. Here Dave used defamatory language that concerned Ellen because he called her "a drug user." Also, the information was published to a third party because Dave made the comment at a board meeting with four others present. Finally, the statement caused damage to the Plaintiff's reputation because she was shunned by other board members and her opinion was quickly discarded at the meeting. Thus, Ellen has a high likelihood of winning a defamation suit against Dave.

Discussion of Model Answer to Exercise C-3

I have only provided one model answer to this exercise. Again, note how the facts match up to various parts of the rule. If you feel comfortable with this format, I urge you to practice it each time you write out an essay. Remember—think of each "issue" as it's own "mini-essay." In this way, writing out an essay (which will have multiple issues) won't seem quite so daunting, and you can more easily stay focused on the task at hand.

Appendix D
What the NCBE Says

I think it's important to know a little about what the people drafting your exam questions have to say. According to the National Conference of Bar Examiners ("NCBE"), the purpose of the MBE is to assess the extent to which an examinee can apply fundamental legal principles and legal reasoning to analyze a given fact pattern. The questions focus on the understanding of legal principles rather than the memorization of substantive law. I have reprinted below the Bar Examiners' guidelines for drafting questions, as noted on their website.

The Guidelines for Drafting MBE Questions

The drafters want to focus items on key concepts and principles that are essential for all examinees to understand, and avoid esoteric topics that are not essential.

The drafters emphasize scenarios that are relevant to practice.

Their task is to develop well-written scenarios that include clear fact patterns.

Finally, their goal is to ensure that the question is asking something important, and that any option requires the examinee to make important distinctions.

Myths about the MBE

According to the NCBE, the following are all UNTRUE myths about the MBE and the bar exam in general:

1. The MBE is a "multiple guess test" for which there are no right answers.

2. If you study only for the MBE and you get a high score, you don't need to worry about the rest of the exam.

3. Bar examiners seek to maximize the number of failing examinees.

4. Passing in July is more likely than in February.

5. Answering 100s upon 100s of MBE questions is all you need to do to be prepared for the MBE.

A few side notes as they relate to the type of questions presented on the MBE. First, according to the NCBE, there are no longer "Roman Numeral" type questions on the MBE. I mention this because you will undoubtedly encounter some sample "Roman Numeral" questions in your practice materials—and they can be tricky. I'm not saying you shouldn't try to answer these types of practice questions, but know that you won't have to deal with them on the actual exam. Here is an example of a "Roman Numeral" question, just so you know what I'm talking about:

MBE SAMPLE QUESTION #8

Able entered into a written contract with Baker to sell Greenacre. The contract was dated June 19 and called for a closing date on the following August 19. There was no other provision in the contract concerning the closing date. The contract contained the following clause: "subject to the purchaser, Baker, obtaining a satisfactory mortgage at the current rate." On the date provided for closing, Baker advised Able that he was unable to close because his mortgage application was still being processed by a bank. Able desired to declare the contract at an end and consulted his attorney in regard to his legal position.

Which of the following are relevant in advising Able of his legal position?

I.   Is time of the essence?
II.   Parol evidence rule.
III. Statute of Frauds.
IV.   Specific performance.

A.   I and III only.
B.   II and IV only.
C.   II, III, and IV only.
D.   I, II, III, and IV.

Additionally, the NCBE has phased out multiple questions based on a single fact pattern. At this point, it is a good bet that such questions are already phased out. Here is an example of how these types of questions are introduced: "Questions 31–32 are based on the following fact pattern." Now, instead of having multiple questions from one fact pattern, each question has its own fact pattern. It's okay to go ahead and do either of these types of questions in your practice sessions, but do know that they won't show up on the actual exam.

If you have any questions, you can contact the NCBE at the address, phone number or email below. Additionally, the NCBE website contains a great deal of information, including sample MBE questions, and comprehensive outlines for each MBE subject. The website address is www.ncbex.org.

National Conference of Bar Examiners
302 S. Bedford Street
Madison, WI 53703-3622
Phone: 608-280-8550
Fax: 608-280-8552
TDD: 608-661-1275

E-mail: contact@ncbex.org

Appendix E
Author's Note and Additional Zen Quotes

It is my sincere hope that this book has helped you on your path to the enlightenment of passing the bar exam. If this book has helped in some way along your path, I would love to hear your feedback (or suggestions for improving the book). Feel free to email me at chadnoreuil@yahoo.com.

I invite you to apply some of the Zen principles I have outlined to your everyday life. I can tell you that the more "present" I am in everyday life, the more enjoyable life is. I leave you with a few additional Zen quotes that may prove helpful in your journey to passing the bar exam, as well as your journey to enlightenment in this lifetime. Peace and positive energy to all....

A student came to
his teacher and said
that he was confused.
He'd been observing his teacher give
counsel now for several months, and it
seemed that the teacher never gave the
same advice. Not only that, he appeared to
give contradictory advice to his students.
The student asked for an explanation, for
he could find none on his own.
The teacher answered, "It's really quite
simple. It's as if I'm looking at each situation
from a perch above, helping others find the
center. Some are to the left, and I tell them
go right; others are to the right, and I tell
them to go left. To those below, I say go up;
to those above, I say go down. The words
are not important — finding our center is all
that matters."

See
value in
what is,
usefulness in what is not.

When we forget
what we should be,
we find what we are.

This moment of your life is a gift—
that's why it's called "The Present."

Student says "I am very discouraged. What should I do?"
Master says, "encourage others."

In all things,
know where to stop.
Sometimes you need to finish before
the end, while other times you must go
beyond where others go. True knowledge
is knowing when to go forward...
and when not to.

When we concern
ourselves with
acquiring or
losing things,
the only thing we truly get is a lack
of inner peace. Yet when we accept
what we have, contentment reigns.

What can we
really control
except our ability to give up the need to control?

The world is a mirror:
What we see is who we are.

Money, fame, and fortune
may further us in our time here, but what of it
will remain at the end of our days? Find what will remain.

Be compassionate.
Be a messenger that delivers compassion to everyone —
not through some esoteric practice, but through the
kindness of your eyes.

You will not be punished for your anger;
you will be punished by your anger.
        — the Buddha

Happiness just _is_.
It isn't something you have to earn, look for,
or wait to receive — it's always there. To find it,
simply stop looking and become it.

When we accept
ourselves completely,
enlightenment happens.

We are what we think. All that we are arises with our thoughts. With our thoughts, we make the world.
— *the Buddha*

The story you tell about your life is the story your life becomes.
— *Dr. John Demartini*
(from "The Breakthrough Experience")

☯   ☯   ☯

I will leave you with this last quote, just in case you missed it at the end of Chapter 2....

Your work is to discover your world
and then with all your heart
give yourself to it.
— *the Buddha*

Index